HIGHER THAN EVEREST

HIGHER THAN EVEREST

TENDI SHERPA:

A LIFETIME OF CLIMBING THE WORLD

FLORE DUSSEY

WHITE OWL

AN IMPRINT OF PEN & SWORD BOOKS LTD.
YORKSHIRE - PHILADELPHIA

First published in Great Britain in 2022 by
Pen & Sword White Owl
An imprint of
Pen & Sword Books Ltd
Yorkshire - Philadelphia

ISBN 978 1 399064 187

Inspired by the book *Tendi Sherpa: Plus haut que l'Everest* by Armand Dussex, published in 2016 (9782839918459)

Typeset in INDIA By IMPEC eSolutions
Printed and bound in England
By CPI (UK) Ltd.

Pen & Sword Books Ltd. incorporates the Imprints of Pen & Sword Archaeology, Atlas, Aviation, Battleground, Discovery, Family History, History, Maritime, Military, Naval, Politics, Railways, Select, Transport, True Crime, Fiction, Frontline Books, Leo Cooper, Praetorian Press, Seaforth Publishing, Wharncliffe and White Owl.

For a complete list of Pen & Sword titles please contact

PEN & SWORD BOOKS LIMITED
47 Church Street, Barnsley, South Yorkshire, S70 2AS, England
E-mail: enquiries@pen-and-sword.co.uk
Website: www.pen-and-sword.co.uk

or

PEN AND SWORD BOOKS
1950 Lawrence Rd, Havertown, PA 19083, USA
E-mail: uspen-and-sword@casematepublishers.com
Website: www.penandswordbooks.com

For Romane Dali, Dolma and Dechen

'Always do your best!'
Liz Schick, 1998

CONTENTS

FOREWORD

TENDI IS A REMARKABLE MAN with an incredible story of how he came to be the professional mountain guide he is today. As a child he grew up in a remote Sherpa village and was sent to study as a child monk at a Buddhist monastery. After five years he left and started working in the trekking business as a teenaged porter, working his way up from there to cook-boy, to *sirdar* (a local responsible for expeditions), to mountaineer, before finally qualifying as an UIAGM certified mountain guide.

His story is one of the wonderful transitions that has occurred for the Nepalese mountain people. In the early days of mountaineering in the Himalayas, the Sherpa climbers had little or no training and had to learn as they went. It was dangerous work and fatalities were frequent. Now, however, the new generation of Nepalese mountaineers are becoming the great guides of the Himalayan peaks; many of them have summited Mount Everest (or Chomolungma/Sagarmatha to give it its Nepalese/Tibetan name) ten or twenty times.

The people carry a confidence and warmth with them that is their trademark, and it is these qualities that my father, Sir Edmund Hillary, found so appealing about the high-country people of Nepal. He never felt sorry for them, despite the hardships of their lives, and respected their wishes as he began to build schools and hospitals they had requested. It was a collaborative approach that galvanised many friendships and kept him returning to the Himalayas; a place he considered a second home. My father's Himalayan Trust team built forty-two schools and hospitals in the Mount Everest region of Nepal, and we continue this work through the Himalayan Trust (www.himalayantrust.org) and other partners.

In the same spirit, in partnership with his own father and another Swiss friend, Tendi started a programme called Nepalko Sathi (Friends of Nepal) to bring infrastructure to the remote valleys, including his old home in the Khembalung Valley. More recently, the Tendi Sherpa Foundation is building schools and training centres and bringing support to the widows of Sherpa mountaineers.

The partnership that my father and Tenzing Norgay shared on Everest, which led to the first ascent of the mountain on 29 May 1953, became known as one of the crowning achievements of the century. Hillary & Tenzing became the "rock stars" of mountaineering and a metaphor for achieving a goal. And what could be a higher goal than climbing Everest?!

I have gone on over fifty expeditions to mountains around the world, including five Everest expeditions on different routes with two summits. And now my two sons, George and Alexander, are being drawn to the mountains. They shared an ascent of the Matterhorn of the Himalayas, Amadablam (6,900 metres), with Tendi, and it was a landmark event for both. Tendi became a true friend and a trusted partner on the mountain.

Tendi is a remarkable man. He is just as at home on an 8,000-metre Himalayan mountainside discussing philosophical questions as he is sitting in a coffee shop sipping a café latte. He exudes a warmth that immediately attracts people to him and has a broad smile that reminds me of Tenzing Norgay, my father's trusted climbing partner.

He truly is a man of Everest.

Peter Hillary

2022

INTRODUCTION

THIS SHORT INTRODUCTION to the Sherpas and their culture aims to provide additional elements of understanding to the reader.

Sherpas

On 29 May 1953, Sir Edmund Hillary and Tenzing Norgay reached the summit of Everest. No one before had ever climbed so high. Tenzing Norgay became a legend, and other Sherpas would follow in the footsteps of this hero, setting all kinds of records. Indeed, most commercial expeditions undertaken in the Himalayas would be impossible without them, whether as guides or porters.

Today, these men, and sometimes women, work far beyond the Himalayan range. Consequently, the term "sherpa" is often used incorrectly and deserves to be clarified.

Definition:

Sherpa (with a capital 'S')
A member of the Sherpa ethnic group, but also the family name of members of this same ethnic group. The women are commonly called Sherpani, but their surname remains Sherpa.

Sherpa (with a capital 'S')
Sherpas have their own language, Sherpa, which is close to Tibetan. However, the language is starting to die out and Nepali is commonly used for commerce and the tourism sector.

sherpa (with a lower-case 's')
The word sherpa is generally used to designate porters, especially since most are from other ethnic groups such as Rais, Tamangs, Gurungs, Magars or Newars. Hindus can also carry out this role. However, summiters and high-altitude workers are mainly Sherpas.

Origins:
Sherpas are members of an ethnic group that migrated from Kham province in eastern Tibet to Nepal, approximately 500 years ago. The word "sherpa" means people (pa) of the east (sher). Due to the lack of any written evidence on the history of the Sherpas, the reason behind their migration is a complex issue and was possibly due to religious or politico-social tensions with the Mongols present in Tibetan territory. The Sherpa people migrated gradually to Nepal, a distance of 2,000 km, from the sixteenth to the eighteenth century, which naturally involved crossing the high Himalayan passes. The first families settled in Khumbu, then in Pharak and Solu, with successive waves also settling in the Rolwaling Valley and as far as the Arun Valley. Meanwhile, other populations settled in Helambu, north of Kathmandu.

Occupations:
Historically, Sherpas lived mainly from agriculture and animal husbandry, growing barley and a variety of millets

(small-seeded cereal crops). The potato, which can be grown up to 4,000 metres above sea level, was introduced by the British in the mid-nineteenth century. This improvement in nutrition had long-lasting effects, with the Sherpa population increasing five-fold in the last 150 years.

Many Sherpas raised yaks, which roamed the high pastures above 5,000 metres. From the first 'Western' mountaineering expeditions to the Himalayas, these men, accustomed to such harsh conditions, constituted the ideal workforce for expeditions and other treks, and have since become true mountain professionals. Tourism has changed their lives considerably. Many have given up farming, drawn by the possibility of the additional benefits that can be gained from this new sector. Some have abandoned their lands completely to settle in Kathmandu, and while some have achieved high-ranking positions such as agency heads, *sirdar*, or owners and operators of lodges on the expedition routes, there are others who must content themselves with more menial roles and lead a miserable life. Indeed, the amount of money earned from four or five expeditions per year is nowhere near enough to live in the capital, where prices are often well above their means.

Castes:

Socially, Nepal is organized hereditarily, according to the Hindu caste system.[1] Marriages are generally arranged between people of the same caste, but of different tribes, with the Brahmin and Chhetri ethnic groups largely dominating

---

[1] Lemaire, S-A., *Organisation de la société népalaise*, Zone Himalaya, A la découverte du Népal et de l'Himalaya (2012) www.zonehimalaya.net/Nepal/moeurs.htm

Nepalese political and intellectual life.[2] Today, however, the Sherpas believe that they can speak as equals with members of these high castes.

Religion:

Sherpas practice the ancient tantric Buddhist religion, also known as Tibetan Buddhism. They honour many deities during rites that punctuate a calendar specific to them, and their festivities aim to attract the favours and protection of these benevolent spirits against other harmful entities.[3] Very superstitious, they believe in the existence of evil spirits here on Earth. Shamanic practices are common, and through trances and rituals, shamans can diagnose illnesses, heal, or practice divination.[4]

There are many monasteries in Sherpa country and it is not only celibate monks who live there, but also married men and women, widows, and widowers. Some settle there permanently, while others only stay there for a few weeks. The clergy is also made up of numerous village *lamas* (priests, single or married, who preside over many Buddhist rituals and festivities punctuating the lives of Sherpas, and who teach Tibetan Buddhism), who officiate in a *gompa* (Buddhist place of worship). They are generally married men and fathers of families who have acquired elementary religious knowledge

---

[2] Béguin, G., Cailmail, B., Durand-Dastès, F., Gaborieau, M., Petech, L., Ramirez, P., *Népal Groupes ethniques et castes*, Universalis (2022) https://www.universalis.fr/encyclopedie/nepal/2-groupes-ethniques-et-castes/$

[3] Hanson, F. A., 'The Semiotics of Ritual', *Semiotica*, 33(1/2), pp. 169-178.

[4] Ortner, S. B., 'The Case of the Disappearing Shamans, or no Individualism, no Relationalism', *Ethos*, 23(3), 355-390 (1995), pp. 357-8.

in order to read mantras and lead religious ceremonies. These men are generally highly respected and thus called upon in the event of illness to chase away evil spirits which, according to them, are the cause of all evil.

In addition to their religious practices, the nuns generally take part in the work of agriculture and animal husbandry, and many single or widowed women join these communities.

Religion is omnipresent in the lives of Sherpas. *Chorten*, or *Stupa* (Buddhist monuments containing relics or sacred texts that sanctify and protect the places they are built), *Mani* walls (stones engraved with Buddhist prayers), windmills and prayer flags line the paths and villages. Each house, meanwhile, has a family altar.

The first Westerners who came to explore the Himalayan peaks discovered a pious people, but they were above all taken back by the exceptional physical qualities of the Sherpas, who have since then provided essential support for all expeditions. Exposed to high altitude for multiple generations, they are particularly well adapted to the harsh living conditions found there and have even adapted genetically as a result. The Sherpa people have a reputation for being brave, tireless and dedicated, and while this is true for many of them, they also experience many of the same issues that other communities have to deal with.

Today, Sherpas live between tradition and modernity. Tendi Sherpa, an internationally recognized mountain guide, constantly moves between these two worlds. Mobile phone in hand, not to mention several thousand followers on social media, he maintains the ability to isolate himself for hours in meditation and his connection to Buddha is, unquestionably, at the heart of his life.

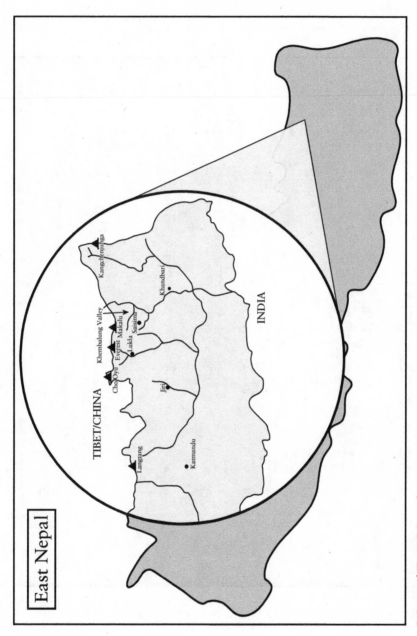

East Nepal

Map of East Nepal.

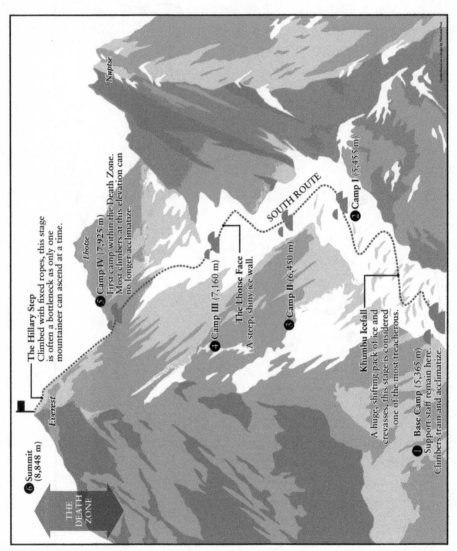

The Hillary Step
Climbed with fixed ropes, this stage is often a bottleneck as only one mountaineer can ascend at a time.

Nuptse

Lhotse

⑤ Camp IV (7,925 m)
First camp within the Death Zone. Most climbers at this elevation can no longer acclimatize.

④ Camp III (7,160 m)

The Lhotse Face
A steep, shiny ice wall.

③ Camp II (6,450 m)

SOUTH ROUTE

② Camp I (5,455 m)

Khumbu Icefall
A huge, shifting pack of ice and crevasses, this stage is considered one of the most treacherous.

① **Base Camp** (5,365 m)
Support staff remain here. Climbers train and acclimatize.

Everest

⑥ Summit (8,848 m)

THE DEATH ZONE

Map showing the ascent of Everest via the south route.

PART ONE

CHAPTER ONE

GABBY'S REMARKABLE FEAT

NO ASCENT IN NEPAL BEGINS without the *puja* ritual; a Buddhist incantation in the mountains, the exact dates of which are dictated by the Tibetan calendar. Tendi Sherpa is always delighted to share this special ceremony with all the teams present at base camp. In the 2022 season, 316 mountaineers have been given permits to climb Everest, 92 fewer than in 2021, a record year. This is rather good news for Tendi, because finding yourself in a crowd on top of the world is not an easy task.

The weather is calm on 19 April, as Westerners and Sherpas gather around the stone *chorten*, some sitting on chairs, others preferring to stand. Tendi takes his two Australian clients, Jane and Gabby, from the organization 'Climbing The Seven Summits' (CTSS), by the arm and whispers in their ear:

'*Puja* always brings me great inner peace. You'll see, it'll take us to the top.'

The *lama* kicks off the ceremony by ringing a bell, its vibrant sound acting as an appeal to the gods. The *puja* allows the climbers to present themselves to the Himalayan mountains in all humility, as the men and women who dream of conquering Everest ask the gods for permission and protection in crossing their otherwise inaccessible kingdom.

Jane closes her eyes and lets herself be invaded by the metallic sound of the cymbals. Meanwhile, Gabby, her 19-year-old daughter, keeps her eyes wide open so as not to miss out on this solemn moment.

Cut flowers and foodstuffs are placed near an altar as offerings, as Tibetan music plays over the reading of mantras; the sacred utterances in Sanskrit that take the form of simple syllables or sentences and possess a particular spiritual power, often used for ritual purposes, protection, invocation as well as meditation. As this is taking place, Tendi sets fire to a juniper branch and incense sticks, reciting prayers as he goes along.

During the ceremony, a pole is erected in the middle of the camp, with dozens of prayer flags emanating from the centre. Spiritual thoughts are imprinted on each square of coloured fabric and when the wind blows, they fly away towards those who need them most. The mountaineers next bring forward their helmets, ice axes, shoes, crampons, ropes and harnesses to be blessed. Some even hand over more personal items, such as their child's comforter.

The two *lamas* pass a *khata* around each person's neck. This prayer scarf, symbolizing good omens and compassion, is traditionally made from white silk and is offered as a sign of benevolence. Next, a red and orange string is added, before the procession ends with the throwing of lucky grains of rice. In the same spirit, Tendi surprises Gabby by rubbing flour on her face. Everyone laughs and starts to do the same. The two hours it has taken to perform the rites will undoubtedly be enough to appease the mountain gods, and thus obtain their permission to climb the 8,000 metres to the top. All signals are go for a good climb.

This is the second time Gabby and Jane have been at Everest base camp. Their adventure had begun when the teenager was just 14 and her father, Jarrod, had asked what her craziest dream was:

'Actually, I'd really like to climb Everest!'

Jarrod replied, tit for tat, 'OK, well you might as well start preparing for it right away.'

Eight weeks later, Gabby and her mother were trekking to the base camp of the mythical Nepalese-Tibetan peak. The young girl walked quickly, adjusting to the altitude remarkably well. As far as Gabby was concerned, growing up meant a life full of sports, and from an early age physical activity had been an integral part of her education, including triathlon, climbing, swimming and indoor gym sessions.

According to Gabby's philosophy, before climbing the highest mountain in the world, you had to prove yourself first. So she began her apprenticeship as a summiter by climbing a 4,000 peak on the Malaysian island of Borneo, in Southeast Asia. Back in Oceania, she rubbed shoulders with the New Zealand mountains through an intensive mountaineering course, her passion for the mountains growing by the day. However, she still lacked the experience of high altitudes, so she returned to Nepal and exceeded 6,000 metres three times, without oxygen, by easily climbing Island Peak with her father. Six months later, she conquered Mera Peak, then the western pass of Baruntse.

That same year, 2019, Gabby entered the history books by becoming the youngest woman to summit the 8,201 metres of Cho Oyu when she was only 16 years old. Her extraordinary achievements were not only relayed at home in Australia, but also in the specialist press.

In spring 2022, Jane agrees to accompany her daughter to Everest. Tendi will be Gabby's official guide, while Jane will team up with Pasang, the Sherpa with whom Gabby climbed Cho Oyu three years earlier. Jane knows that her daughter is in good hands with Tendi. Before embarking on the adventure, Mike Hamill, the director of CTSS, had spoken to her at length about the extraordinary abilities of this 38-year-old Nepalese man who had worked for him for many years.

After several weeks of acclimatization, the assault on Mount Everest can finally begin. Before leaving base camp, however, Gabby addresses one of her sponsors in a video that she immediately posts on social media:

'Hey, Belle. Hey, Sam. I hope everything's good back in Australia. I'm definitely missing home, but I'm super excited to be here. Mum's also smashing it, which is great! I just wanted to say thanks again for all the support you guys have provided to help bring my dream to life.'

At 6 am on 10 May, the two parties leave base camp (5,365m), hoping that four days later they will reach 8,848m and have climbed the highest mountain in the world. Tendi has devoted time to help his young client mentally prepare for what is to come. First, he explained each of the risks involved: the dangers of ice climbing, the risk of avalanches, the cold, managing fatigue, the lack of sleep and oxygen, before finally moving into the death zone above 8,000m. He then tried to get to the bottom of what it was that motivated her to do this. Trying to find answers within yourself is never easy and usually stirs up plenty of emotion, so it is with a trembling voice that Gabby recounts her school years where her self-confidence was often very low. Tendi understands that sometimes, in order to fulfill oneself, you have to prove to certain people what you're capable of, almost as a rite of passage. Besides, when Gabby makes a promise, she goes to great lengths to keep it, not just for her, but for her parents, who have committed huge resources to this expedition, and for all those who have supported her both emotionally and financially in her quest. She sees it as her duty to succeed.

The ability of her guide to listen to what she says touches Gabby deeply. Indeed, during the last phone call to her father before beginning the ascent, she told him:

'Don't worry, Dad. I have complete faith in Tendi. I feel like he knows me better than anyone. It's like he can read my mind. He's an absolute pro and will take good care of me. I'm so lucky to have him by my side.'

In the endless climb to the top, Jane starts to suffer from the altitude but continues to fulfill her role as mother, friend, confidante, and coach. Although the pair were already very close, a new bond has now been woven between mother and daughter. Jane knows that her eldest daughter suffers from the absence of her siblings, her friends, and Monty, her dog. Despite this, she also knows that Gabby is sufficiently armed to overcome this ordeal, even though not so very long ago she was still only a schoolgirl.

On the day of the final assault, the famous summit push, the Jane/Pasang team go on ahead of Tendi and Gabby, who set off from the South Col two hours later, at 9 pm. The duo moves at an impressive pace, passing many other top contenders as they work their way upwards. The last 850 metres of elevation are thus travailed in darkness, for several hours, before the four climbers come together just before the summit ridge. With oxygen masks fixed to their faces, the two Nepalese guides, accompanied by their three support

Sherpas and the two Australians, progress without speaking, concentrating everything they have on their breathing. As Jane digs deep inside herself to face this extreme challenge, Gabby feels more connected to the mountains than ever before. She is amazed at her strength and is even pleased that the training she acquired attending all those parties with friends in Melbourne, which were followed the next day by either intense classes at school or sports activities, have prepared her for the experience of sleepless nights!

At 4.30 am on Saturday, 14 May, Gabby throws herself into Jane's arms, as the tears start to flow. Mother and daughter have reached the highest point on the planet, and Gabby has consequently become the youngest Australian to have climbed Everest. Tendi and Pasang congratulate their clients with warm hugs as the day begins to break around them, offering a unique spectacle: from a deep hyacinth blue, the sky momentarily passes through infinite shades of the same colour, and with each passing second, the palette evolves, tracing a thin orange streak on the horizon. Hundreds of white peaks appear below them, as far as the eye can see. There are no clouds and not even the slightest breath of wind. Luckily, the crowds of people seen on the summit in previous years are not here this time, meaning selfies and photos can be taken from all angles.

Jane takes off her mask for a moment to congratulate Tendi, who has just completed his fourteenth summit of Everest. He smiles at her in thanks, before moving a few steps away from the group; for him, this is not a moment for personal glory. His mind is turned towards contemplation and despite the ambient –20°C (–4°F) temperature, he takes off his glove and extracts a small, air-tight tube from his pocket. He unscrews it, closes his eyes, takes a deep breath, and recites a mantra. In complete communion, he raises the cylinder above his head and lets the ashes of his North American client, who died in his arms a few months ago on the slopes of Manaslu, slip away in the icy wind. Out loud, he says: 'It was your dream to get here. Now you're home. May your soul rest in peace, my dear friend.' Once this sacred act has been accomplished, the guide returns to the small group.

For more than twenty minutes, Gabby, Jane, Pasang, Tendi and a few other Sherpas from the team stand on the tiny summit platform in this environment that is as magical as it is inhospitable. However, it is impossible to stay any longer without putting their lives at risk. Once back at the South Col, Jane and Pasang will continue their descent while Gabby, guided by Tendi and an iron will, makes the ascent of the nearby Lhotse, the fifth highest mountain in the world (8,516m). In achieving this feat, this 19-year-old young woman will show a strength, courage and determination that Tendi has never encountered before.

CHAPTER TWO

ON THE SLOPES OF MANASLU

TENDI LOOKS AT HIS ALTIMETER. The 8,000-metre mark is not very far away, but there are still 150 metres of elevation to go before reaching the summit of Manaslu. The sun has just risen and conditions for climbing are perfect. Suddenly, Tendi's North American client, who's been in great shape so far, sits down, takes a few breaths, then rocks back. The guide realizes that something is terribly wrong. He grabs him by the jacket, calls out his name, shakes him. No answer. He takes his pulse. Nothing. No heartbeat. Cheten, the second Sherpa who's there to assist Tendi, immediately readjusts the client's oxygen mask to increase the air supply. But it has no effect: the client is on the ground, unconscious. Without thinking about the difficulty of what he is undertaking, Tendi begins cardiac massage. The temperature is around –20°C (–4°F) and because the man is wearing a huge down jacket, it is impossible to release the chest properly. Wedged down into the slope, Tendi pushes his palms into the client's chest at the gruelling rate of 100 beats per minute. At 8,000 metres above sea level, it is impossible for anyone to maintain such a pace and, after ten long minutes, the guide is forced to stop, exhausted. He collapses next to the lifeless body feeling, for the first time in his life, abandoned by the gods. His thoughts spiral down a black hole. Images clash and collide with each other in his mind. Blurred visions of his wife, Phuru, and his two little daughters, Dolma and Dechen, appear before his eyes and it is impossible to see clearly. Tendi cannot believe it. He does not understand how, in a few seconds, everything could have changed.

There are few expedition companies who have never had to deal with a death at high altitude. Each mountaineer reacts differently to cold, wind and especially to the lack of oxygen. In order to be best prepared to face these extreme conditions, about sixty days is essential for acclimatization, during which time the human body will increase its production of red blood cells. However, for this metabolism to be successful, a person must spend more than four weeks living between 5,000 and 7,000 metres above sea level.

Since the start of commercial expeditions, just under 6,000 people have reached the summit of Everest, while 300 have lost their lives on its slopes. The mortality rate is even higher on other 8,000-metre peaks, such as K2 and Annapurna (according to a survey by Mountain IQ, the mortality rate on Annapurna is 27 percent). Around 85 climbers have perished on Manaslu, and Tendi's client is now part of this horrible statistic. Warning signs appear in the vast majority of deaths, the most common being confusion, the inability to continue walking, vomiting and, of course, extreme fatigue.

During their careers, Tendi and Mike Hamill (Tendi's employer and himself a great Himalayan mountaineer), have witnessed many dramas played out in the mountains, including several cases of climbers succumbing to sudden heart failure. Yet it is still a shock to face a sudden death like this. Indeed, there had been no warning signs at all as the client had not shown the slightest sign of weakness until the moment he succumbed.

Several minutes pass before Cherten signals to Tendi that he needs get up and pull himself together:

'Tendi, get moving, damn it! We can't stay here! We have to leave immediately or we'll put ourselves in danger!'

Tendi draws on his deepest resources, those taught to him by the *lama* of his village, when Tendi attended a school for young monks. The holy man confided to him: 'When stress invades you and you are at your worst, breathe and think of nothing but the spirit of Buddha'. He takes a deep breath through his oxygen mask and then exhales slowly. Meanwhile, Cherten pulls up the dead man's hood to cover his face. Tendi, who has finally come to his senses, makes a harness that will allow them to carry this 90-kilogram body down to the next lower camp, and the macabre group begins its descent.

When a fatality occurs in the death zone, very strict rules are applied. In principle, the body must remain in place and all accompanying persons must go to the next equipped camp before notifying the head of the agency of the situation. The latter then has the unfortunate task of informing the families, not to mention discussing with the insurance companies whether they will take care of the body's removal. After all, the evacuation of a dead body is a very challenging and dangerous procedure at nearly 8,000 metres above sea level: helicopters are unable to fly at those heights, meaning five or six porters are needed for such an undertaking. When they do take place, operations like this are long and risky.

Even though Tendi knows these rules perfectly well, he decides not to apply them. He has seen too many corpses abandoned on the slopes of Everest and refuses to leave the client's remains on the hostile slopes of Manaslu. But carrying a lifeless body is no easy task.

After reaching Camp 4, Tendi and his assistant find Tenji Sherpa, a star in the world of mountaineering who is preparing to climb Manaslu in the fastest time ever achieved. But glory will have to wait. Without hesitation, the athlete abandons his quest and agrees to lend a hand to his friend, Tendi.

The two guides are both experienced in conducting rescue operations in extreme conditions. They start by protecting the body in a sleeping bag, then place it on several insulating blankets and strap everything together to form a makeshift stretcher. Next begins the interminable descent, which will last thirteen hours. Right from the start, the two men face a steep slope of fifty degrees. The stretcher is difficult to handle. Tenji takes his place at the front, Tendi at the back, as they slide it along the fixed ropes using a descender. Every 30 metres they must redo a belay and fix the lowering system again.

The major problem, however, is the large number of climbers on the fixed rope that was put in place by the high-altitude Sherpas. Most of the different expeditions on the mountain began their climbs at the same time owing to the favourable weather window for the summit push, and at each cross over point on the fixed ropes, the stretcher risks obstructing those on their way up. The consequence of a mistake is inconceivable, and the two guides must increase their efforts to control the downward trajectory of the improvised stretcher. When they pull alongside some of the climbers on the rope, the foreign mountaineers remain silent and look away. Tenji and Tendi are on their own.

The route flattens out, so Tendi and Tenji change positions. Standing side by side, they both pull the stretcher from the front. At 9 pm, in the cold, dark night, the illuminated tents of Camp 3 finally appear. Exhausted, the two men collapse into their tent and sleep until sunrise. The next morning, despite the deteriorating weather, the Kailash helicopter lands and Tendi hoists the stretcher inside the machine.

The procedures are identical for each death at altitude: the police carry out the usual checks and draw up a death certificate. The body is then taken to Kathmandu University Hospital to identify the causes of death, while the embassy usually takes care of repatriation.

When he arrives back home, Tendi confesses to his wife that he is no longer sure he wants to continue working as a guide. She listens, reassuring him that he has absolutely nothing to reproach himself for. Khamsu, Tendi's father, prays for the memory of the client, but also for his son so that he may quickly regain his confidence and faith in his profession.

CHAPTER THREE

NO PENGUINS

TENDI OFTEN THINKS ABOUT HIS late client's parents. Is there anything worse in the world than losing a child? Since the recent tragedy, a certain emptiness in the soul occasionally takes over his otherwise eternal *joie de vivre*. However, the comfort of his family and acts of meditation soothes him little by little and the knot in his stomach slowly disappears.

The tragic accident on Manaslu has reminded him how dangerous his job is. The reality envelopes him more and more that if anything bad were to happen to him, his wife would be financially unable to raise their two daughters. But Phuru is not the only one relying on Tendi's income. Among the Sherpas, the eldest son must take care of all relatives in need and for Tendi, the list is long. His parents, Khamsu and Dali, have no pension (there is none available in Nepal), while an elderly aunt, who has remained in their home village of Saisima, relies solely on her nephew. Nima, his younger brother, lives in a monastery thanks to the generous donations of his older brother. And he occasionally helps two of his cousins who are unable to find work.

A qualified mountain guide earns a good living, but only when he is on an expedition. In Nepal, government unemployment benefits do not exist. What is more, the first months of the Coronavirus pandemic in 2020 plunged Tendi into the most agonizing of uncertainties. Tourists deserted the

Himalayas seemingly overnight as foreign companies packed up and left. Yet the expenses of maintaining his extended family naturally continued as they had before.

Being confined to the house, however, allowed him to devote more time to his daughters and to keep an eye on his father. Khamsu, now in his early sixties, is still a *bon vivant*, even if he does have a bit of a paunch. As a holy man, he regularly officiates at weddings and takes great joy in these ceremonies, especially the alcohol-fuelled parties that follow. Tendi, on the other hand, does not drink. While it is true that Khamsu is only an occasional drinker, all it takes is for a friend to offer him a *raksi* (a strong, clear drink similar to Japanese sake), for him go beyond drinking in moderation. With skill, the son manages to steer his father away from such temptations.

Tendi is also worried about his eldest daughter. Since the start of the pandemic, the semi-private school that Dolma attends has only been teaching remotely, although the price of her school fees, naturally, is unchanged. The internet connection is poor and at 7 years old, the little girl can no longer bear so many hours spent in front of a computer screen. Stuck at home, with no direct contact with her classmates and teachers, her grades are starting to drop as she spends hours playing games she has downloaded to her mother's phone. Tendi looks for possible solutions in all directions, but to no avail, until some Swiss friends offer to finance private lessons. At the end of summer 2021, a young Sherpani (a woman of Sherpa ethnicity) teacher, who lost her job due to the health crisis, has been helping Dolma at home, five days a week.

After a trying year, both mentally and financially, CTSS, the company Tendi has been working for four years, hires him for an expedition to Antarctica. For Mike Hamill, the company's director, Tendi's experience is highly valuable, especially since he has climbed most of the highest peaks on the seven continents. Not only has he ascended Everest, of course, but also Aconcagua in South America, Kilimanjaro in Africa, Mount Kosciuszko in Oceania and now here he is on his way to Mount Vinson in Antarctica. Even though it might be simpler, from an administrative point of view, for Mike to hire only North American guides, like himself, he always prefers to have Tendi onboard. While many guides can match him in terms of technical ability, few have developed the empathy that Western clients so appreciate, especially when they are exhausted and are forced to draw on their last resources.

So, in December 2021, it is all systems go for Tendi to join Team CTSS at the southern end of the planet. The only setback: in order to travel from Nepal to Antarctica (via the United States), Tendi has to pass more than fifteen Covid tests on the way to Antarctica and, being terribly superstitious, fears that one of them will end up testing positive. But he need not have worried. Luck seems to have smiled on him once again.

The long flight from Punta Arenas in Chile to the Union Glacier is spent looking out of the aircraft window, as a palette of different shades of white parade past for hours on end. After a quick stop, a Twin Otter airplane transports the expedition members to Mount Vinson base camp. CTSS has planned three guides for twelve adventurers. In this inhospitable polar region on the world's most remote continent, expeditions only take place from December to January, the austral summer, although even that is purely relative since temperatures can still get down to −30°C (−22°F).

Tendi would have loved to see penguins and show the photographs to Dolma and little Dechen. But no other living beings make an appearance during the three weeks they spend at the end of the world. There is no flora or fauna in this hostile environment. Nevertheless, it must be respected. That is why all waste is brought back, including human waste, otherwise it would remain in the polar landscape forever.

Equipped with touring skis, a long column of skiers glide across the immaculate snow towards the summit. Everyone pulls a sled carrying all the necessary equipment and supplies needed for total autonomy. Mike can count on the extraordinary physical resilience of Tendi: few guides are able to keep going for so long in such extreme cold. Indeed, during these trips his fitness means he is able to carry loads of up to 35kg.

Isolated as they are, the expedition team bonds quickly. Tendi has a special ability to adapt instantly to the different cultures of his clients. He has mastered both the art of British sarcasm and the principle Japanese rites. And so, in a festive and communal spirit, Christmas Eve takes on a rather special tone. Small gifts are exchanged under an improvised tree made from ski poles, and with his legendary humor, the man from Nepal entertains the group in the light of the midnight sun, since at this time of year, darkness never falls.

On 26 December, the first team reach the summit of Mount Vinson, 4,892 metres above sea level. For logistical reasons, Tendi will actually climb from the base camp to the highest point in Antarctica three times in just eleven days. Despite everything, each member of the expedition has embarked on their own incredible inner journey and Tendi accompanies his clients in his first ascent with humility.

Far from his homeland, Tendi immerses himself in this hostile environment, which he nevertheless considers soothing. Indeed, an unspeakable force emanates from the endless expanse of snow and ice. Eyes closed against the icy wind, the guide begins to meditate. He visualizes the terrestrial globe, seeing himself at its extremity, with Buddha standing by his side. Since the early days of his childhood, prayer has always given rhythm to his life and the practice allows him to renew his tremendous sources of energy every day. He feels grateful for all the extraordinary things he has in his life, often thinking to himself that when it all comes to an end, he will take nothing but the karma he has earned throughout his busy time on Earth.

Back in Kathmandu, his wife and daughters throw him a little party. He has missed his mother's excellent dahl bat (a dish consisting of white rice and a bowl of lentil soup) immensely. He cradles his youngest, Dechen, who is now sixteen months old, then spends hours playing hide and seek with Dolma. Phuru, his young wife, listens to his stories attentively, admiring her husband. She is always delighted each time he comes home.

CHAPTER FOUR

THE RUSH TO EVEREST

ON 22 MAY 2019, NIRMAL PURJA MAGAR took a photograph that would be seen all around the world, showing nearly 300 people in single file on the summit ridge of Everest. What a sight! A traffic jam right in the middle of the death zone – what could be more bizarre? Ten mountaineers would lose their lives during this particular edition of the climbing "window", but the Nepalese government categorically rejected any accusations related to over-crowding.

Twenty-four hours after his friend Nims had taken the image, Tendi photographed the same kind of crowd near the summit of Everest. It should be noted that conditions that year were absolutely appalling, with the good weather window being substantially reduced. This meant that in order to succeed in the ascent, everyone had to begin at the same time. For several years Tendi had noticed that the number of candidates had been constantly increasing, while the number of days of good weather was going in the opposite direction.

With only one client, a 62-year-old American spine surgeon called Ed Dohring, Tendi believes they will be able make swift progress. This was, in fact, the American's second attempt at Everest, having been forced to turn around due to bad weather after reaching 8,400 metres on his previous endeavour. With experience of climbing at altitude, he has certainly been climbing well up until this point.

As the rope team reach the Balcony at the significant altitude of 8,500 metres, an endless column of climbers stands before them at a complete standstill. How many people are there waiting motionless in the freezing cold? Tendi can't believe what he is seeing and fears the worst. As soon as the body stops moving, the effect of the extreme temperatures begins to take hold even more. Sometimes it can go down to −40°C (−40°F), while windspeeds can reach up to 130kmph (80mph). What is more, the oxygen reserves they carry do not account for these long downtimes, so if the wait is too long then they risk running out.

"Hanging around" in the death zone is simply out of the question, so Tendi asks Ed if he feels able to put in a monumental effort to allow them to overtake this long line of humanity. Without hesitation, the doctor nods his head. He has complete confidence in his guide – after all, Tendi has been climbing Everest for fifteen years. Slightly increasing his client's oxygen supply, the Sherpa pulls out his ice axe and unhooks himself from the fixed rope to which all the mountaineers are connected. Instead, he forms an independent rope with Ed and, one following the other, they overtake all those who are stuck on the fixed rope.

Thanks to this alpine technique, the pair manage to progress relatively quickly, although Tendi is very careful not to stray too far from the main, fixed rope. Even though it allows increased mobility, a strategy such as this is only possible for two people, and at this altitude, a guide needs to watch over their client constantly. However, Tendi notices that along the endless queue this is not always the case, and many foreigners are attempting to advance alone, without any close assistance. At such high altitude, a guide needs to ensure their client is breathing correctly through their oxygen mask, that they are sufficiently hydrated, are warm enough, and still have a clear mind. Some less scrupulous agencies accept two or more clients per Sherpa, meaning some climbers can find themselves alone in the death zone. Pure madness!

Arriving at the summit of Everest is not exactly the great moment of happiness that Ed was hoping for. Indeed, the flat part at the top is hardly wider than two table tennis tables placed side by side, and he is immediately jostled by about fifteen other people, each one clambering to find the perfect angle to take a selfie. The surgeon experiences a mix of emotions; from the pride of having accomplished such a life-affirming feat, to the fear of risking that very same life in the middle of this absurd crush. He sits down and simply holds up a banner that reads, 'Hi Mom, love you!' as Tendi takes his photograph and immortalizes the moment. A few days later, the image would appear on the front page of the *International Herald Tribune*, as well as in *The New York Times*.

Shortly after leaving the summit, Tendi and Ed encounter a female climber lying still on the ground, with no guide or other mountaineer anywhere to be seen. They check the body carefully, but it is clear that she is dead, even though she is still connected to the fixed rope by a carabiner. Faced with this appalling scene, a testimony to the great dangers linked to such high altitudes, they have no choice but to step over the body and continue their descent. Ed is sad and disgusted at what he has seen, and after arriving back in Kathmandu would later describe his feelings to several major Western news outlets, including the BBC, CBS and *The New York Times*.

Less than a year later, in March 2020, most countries throughout the world are barricading themselves in to limit the circulation of Coronavirus. Nepal is no exception. Tendi and his team are in the midst of preparing for a new expedition to the roof of the world. The equipment has just been purchased, the porters and guides hired. But suddenly, overnight, everything comes to a halt. No ascent is possible, neither on Everest nor elsewhere. Nevertheless, the director of CTSS manages to pay most of the Sherpas who had already been preparing for the expedition for the past month, and Tendi promises them that the following year, everything will be back to normal. Usually so optimistic, the guide is, in fact, terrified, convinced that the whole world will soon be contaminated with this deadly virus.

After a long, blank year, Nepal finally relaxes its quarantine rules and reopened its borders in 2021. The effect is immediate. In April that year, the government issues a record 408 climbing permits for Everest. As a result, more than 1,000 people can be found at base camp that year. After all, in addition to the climbers, there are also all the support staff (logistics, kitchen, medical teams, weather service etc.) who camp at the foot of the legendary mountain. At 5,365 metres above sea level, Everest base camp is a wonderful bubble of civilization, with each expedition having its own quarters. The CTSS HQ can be seen from afar: a gigantic white igloo-shaped tent housing a comfortable common room complete with ottomans, rugs, table football, and decorated in a Zen-like style. There is even music in the background to help promote relaxation.

The other expedition companies have also set up cozy little nests for their clients. There are film screenings, places to practice yoga or lift dumbbells, warm showers, and even slow, but manageable, WiFi. Fresh produce is transported by yaks and helicopters, and climbers can enjoy Japanese, Italian or Indian cuisine, or just a simple hamburger.

The number of expedition companies in Nepal has boomed since the 1980s, with more than 200 currently registered in Kathmandu. Prices can be up to $100,000 for a VIP package, while the cheaper agencies offer ascents for 'as little as' $20,000. Regardless of the final cost, each figure includes the $11,000 required by the Nepalese government for the permit to climb Everest. Some agencies accept all types of clients, many of whom are inexperienced and have no technical knowledge: it is not uncommon for foreigners to approach the formidable icefall without ever having put crampons on their feet before. Tendi has always struggled to understand how someone can attempt to climb Everest without having subjected their body to the rigorous test required. In Europe, various 4,000-metre peaks allow you to experience the first sensations of what happens to your body when it starts to run out of oxygen. Westerners who want to be even more prepared can practice on other peaks between 5,800 and 7,000 metres, such as Kilimanjaro in Africa (5,895m), Denali in Alaska (6,190m), Aconcagua in South America (6,961m), or a "smaller" Himalayan mountain such as Cho Oyo in Nepal (8,188m). Tendi is happy that the company he works for only accepts well-prepared clients. There is also an additional guarantee: no one leaves for Nepal without the green light from their doctor.

Over the course of his long career, Tendi has heard too many mountaineers say: 'I'm going to reach the top of Everest, even if they have to amputate my fingers and toes!' Faced with such inappropriate assertions, Tendi always encourages his clients to take the time to appreciate the extraordinary beauty of the mountains and not to make the summit their only motivation. Sadly, the answer is often the same: 'I'm not here as a tourist, the only important thing for me is to get to the top.' As a Buddhist, Tendi never tries to contradict his Western clients, but rather encourages them to approach things differently.

During the 2021 window, which obviously takes place while the pandemic is still active, Tendi supervises the ascent of eight clients, each person climbing with an assigned Sherpa. All members of the group arrive at base camp vaccinated and masked, having been submitted to repeated Covid tests beforehand. Before leaving base camp, the various teams are given updates by meteorologists, who predict that there will be stormy skies for several days. By the time they reach Camp 4 (7,900m), the experts tell Tendi the windspeeds will be 45kmph (28mph). He leaves the tent for a moment to consult his pocket anemometer: it is already showing 62kmph, which is difficult to manage at such an altitude.

However, despite the high winds, the sky is cloudless, and he looks up at the summit of Chomolungma (Everest in Sherpa), speaking to the mountain in his head, asking if he can continue the climb with his team. An inner voice whispers to him saying no, don't do it! It is always hard to be so close to the goal and have to give up, but, as calmly as he can, he explains to the eight clients that reaching the summit is impossible under such conditions. The tents are already being buffeted violently in the wind, and for Tendi, no one should put themselves in the death zone with such gusts. Nevertheless, as they prepare to leave, he sees groups setting off for their summit push. In total, more than 100 people will attempt the climb in 2021 and although there would be no fatalities, several people would return with severe frostbite. None of Tendi's clients hold it against him for stopping their dreams of climbing Everest from coming true. Everyone fully understands that an expedition leader must be able to put an end to a project of such magnitude when the risks are so high.

Tendi has addressed the Ministry of Tourism several times to request a formal limitation to the number of permits issued. The Association of Nepalese Mountain Guides, of which he is an active member, feel like it is flogging a dead horse. Yet their main demand is very simple: only issue permits to foreigners who already have previous experience climbing high mountains. So far, however, the government has not moved on its position.

If endless queues once again formed on the southern Nepalese side of the roof of the world in 2021, it was because China had continued to keep its access to the Tibetan side of Everest closed due to the pandemic: a consequence of the "zero Covid" policy advocated by Beijing since the start of the crisis. During the 2021 season, Tendi would remain concerned about the threat of he and his team contracting the virus. After all, breathing is hard enough at high altitudes, so having coughing fits, a fever, and an aching body would seriously complicate the situation. Even though Tendi's team did not experience an outbreak of Covid, it still managed to affect 100 people at base camp and beyond, resulting in a succession of helicopters being called to evacuate the most severely affected climbers.

CHAPTER FIVE

SOAP OPERA ON EVEREST

SITTING IN BUSINESS CLASS ON Turkish Airlines, Tendi lowers his surgical mask for a moment to take a selfie, before immediately posting the image on social media. It is the first time he has travelled in such comfort, and he finds it greatly amusing. It was sheer luck that he had managed to find such a bargain whilst looking for a flight from Kathmandu to Geneva, otherwise he would never have dared to take an overpriced flight when someone else was paying. Yet here he is, in August 2021, on his way to being the guest of honour at the International Alpine Film Festival (FIFAD) in Les Diablerets, Switzerland. His great friend Nicolas Bossard picks him up at Geneva airport in his van, which often serves as his makeshift home. Rocking the adventurer look, complete with stubble and sunglasses poised on top of his head, the 30-something is delighted to be reunited with his expedition partner.

Arriving in Montreux, Tendi confesses to Nicolas that he has never been on a boat before, so the two friends jump on the steamship *La Suisse* for a short, impromptu cruise on Lake Geneva between Chillon Castle and Vevey. It has been a long time since Tendi has played the tourist. Afterwards, the winding climb along the beautiful mountain road up to the Vaud resort of Les Diablerets makes his stomach churn a little, even though he is quite used to the "impassable" roads of Nepal.

On reaching the village, Tendi is greeted with admiration and respect, and the room for the evening screening of 'Telenovela on Everest' ('Soap Opera on Everest') is packed. Dressed in casual clothes, caps pulled down on their heads, Tendi and Nicolas head up onto the stage. The Nepalese guide issues a warm *'namaste'* ('hello' in Nepali) to his audience, his aura exuding such benevolence that everyone in the crowd is convinced the greeting is for them personally.

When asked about his achievements, Tendi replies in fluent French, 'I've done quite a few expeditions to Everest, but have only been to the top thirteen times,' much to the audience's delight. 'Next spring,' he continues, 'I'm hoping to make it fourteen. Apart from that, I've climbed Cho Oyu twice, Manaslu three times, Lhotse once and Ama Dablam twice. As for the slightly smaller mountains, I've been to Aconcagua seven times and Kilimanjaro twice. I also like the Swiss mountains – Nicolas and I plan to do the Matterhorn at the end of the week!'

The festival director asks Nicolas to talk about the idea behind 'Telenovela on Everest', and the young director explains that Tendi had offered him the chance to follow one of his clients during his ascent of Everest from the Tibetan side. This was back in 2016, when for the first time in his career, Tendi would be leading an expedition without the slightest involvement from any foreign agency. It would be 100 percent Made in Nepal. Nicolas continues by explaining this meant the pressure on Tendi was enormous. There was absolutely no room for error!

The group who would embark on the expedition included two Malaysians, one Canadian, one Mexican and four Argentinians, including Facundo Arana, the Argentinian TV star. Before leaving Switzerland, Nicolas had searched for his name on Google and discovered a clip of the actor languidly kissing a young woman, although it would appear the sequence had been filmed in slow motion. According to Wikipedia, Facundo was approaching his fifties and was an artist and musician (he plays the saxophone), but there was no comment, however, on any previous alpine adventures.

As the lights in the festival tent begin to dim, the audience hears the sound of sustained breathing through an oxygen mask on the black screen in front of them. Next, an ultra-high-definition image reveals Tendi and Facundo Arana emerging a few hundred metres from the summit. As the actor lowers his mask to address the camera, he thanks his guide for giving him the opportunity to fulfill his life-long dream.

The film then proceeds to retrace the Argentinian's journey on the mythical mountain, beginning at Lhasa, where acclimatization usually lasts for about forty days. Due to a busy schedule, however, Facundo has had little time for training. Nevertheless, he remains convinced that his mental strength will allow him to reach the summit. For him, Everest represents more than a challenge; it is a necessity, an old score he has to settle with himself. During an interview with the actor at base camp, Nicolas confesses he does not share the same desire, reminding him that he is not prepared to risk his life just to shoot a few frames of him on the roof of the world. The star says nothing, but nods his head in understanding.

As they reach 7,000 metres, Facundo finds himself constantly using his oxygen mask, while Tendi spends a great deal of time encouraging him and cheering him on. He congratulates him on arriving at the final camp before nightfall, even if their rate of progress is beginning to worry him. Facundo reassures everyone that he still feels in great shape, but suggests he leaves two hours before the others during their summit push. Nicolas therefore has a two-hour window behind Tendi and the Argentinian. The director knows he can easily catch up with them, even without the assistance of a porter and with 15 kilos of equipment on his back. In the end, he passes them before daybreak and decides to wait 100 metres higher up so he can take a magnificent shot of their ascent, framed by the fiery colours of the breaking dawn. However, despite the short distance separating him from the two climbers, the wait turns out to be too long: he does not want to hang around in the death zone.

Without realizing it, Nicolas reaches the summit of Everest at 10.30 am, half an hour after the "deadline" set by Tendi for the whole group (for security reasons, an expedition leader always sets a deadline for reaching the summit). After 10 am the climbers were supposed to turn back, even if they only had 100 metres to go. While waiting for Facundo, Nicolas takes some shots of the Malaysians and the Canadian as they arrive at the summit, and as the long minutes tick by on the roof of the world, the Mexican is also nearing the goal. Yet there is still no sign of Facundo. At that precise moment, Nicolas has only one concern: fearing he is going to run out of oxygen while waiting, he wants to descend as quickly as possible. With only one spare canister in his bag, he tells himself that a shot of an actor on top of the world is not worth losing his life for. So, without any second thought, he sets off back down again. Below, on the north ridge, he finally comes across Tendi and Facundo. The men are unable to communicate because of the oxygen masks screwed to their faces, but the Argentinian gestures for him to start filming and addresses the camera: 'Look where he's [Tendi] brought me! He's a friend for life.'

The director points out the absurdity of recording an interview at an altitude of 8,800 metres, when every second spent there counts. Yet Facundo does not seem to realize that in order to get these few images, the cameraman is drawing on his last reserves of oxygen. Instead, the Argentinian admits to being a little disappointed that Nicolas did not wait for him at the top, as planned.

After this, Tendi and Facundo continue their laborious ascent to the summit. To save time, Tendi carries out tasks that clients would usually do themselves: every 20 metres, he unhooks the carabiner holding Facundo to the fixed rope, placing him beyond the successive safety anchors set up by the high-altitude climbing Sherpas. They finally reach the summit at 11.30 am. The actor is exhausted. Without dramatizing, Tendi turns to him and says calmly, 'Facu, we can't stay here. If we stay here, we'll die.'

During his descent, Nicolas comes across several corpses frozen in the ice, the macabre encounters serving as a graphic reminder of where he is. Twenty-four hours after his departure, after reaching the advanced camp at 6,500 metres, he starts to become seriously worried. Tendi, Facundo and the rest of the group are still in the death zone. Unbeknownst to him, after arriving at the summit too late, they have had no choice but to spend an extra night at the unrecommended altitude. After a comparative rest, Tendi climbs out of his tent and observes the valley below. The sun is shining in the cloudless sky, and a light breeze caresses his face. He quickly shakes his clients awake and forces them to set off immediately; a storm is coming. A few hours later, while they are sheltered in Camp 3, they are buffeted by strong gusts of wind, and Facundo congratulates Tendi for his remarkable foresight while the weather was still glorious.

After sixty endless hours, the latecomers finally arrive at the advanced camp. The actor is on the verge of exhaustion and admits to having completely underestimated what his body would go through. Tendi feels relieved. Everyone is finally back safe and sound, with the added bonus of having experienced the glory of summiting Everest. Nevertheless, Tendi does admit to having had a few scares along the way... Everest takes people to their limit!

CHAPTER SIX

IN THE FOOTSTEPS OF SIR EDMUND HILLARY

AS A CHILD, TENDI HAD been brought up on the wonderful stories of Sir Edmund Hillary and Tenzing Norgay. He would sit and listen to his father for hours as he told him about the first ascent of Everest. Indeed, on 27 October 1993, Tendi's tenth birthday, Khamsu had taken his son by the hand, led him to the fireside and said: 'Tendi, today is your birthday, and my gift to you is a story I think you'll love and remember for the rest of your life.'

As he settled down, eager to hear the tale, his father began to speak.

'Thirty years before you were born, even before I was born, a New Zealand mountaineer, a Sherpa, like us, reached the summit of Chomolungma.'

Khamsu continued to describe the huge convoy that left Kathmandu at the beginning of March 1953, as seven tons of equipment were transported to the foot of Everest by 350 porters. Several countries had already organized expeditions to reach the summit, but each time the mountaineers had been forced to give up, sometimes only a few hundred metres from their goal. That year, in 1953, the British had decided to try their luck again. This time, a group of seasoned New Zealand climbers, including a certain Edmund Hillary, were to accompany them.

The young Tendi was fascinated by every detail of the expedition, as his father proceeded to tell him about each person's role at the different camps. He told him how important each acclimatization stage was for everyone, then explained the difficulty of picking out routes in the heart of the dangerous Khumbu Icefall.

'Just imagine! Around thirty Sherpas crossing those huge crevasses carrying around 20 kilos on their backs! They had to get down on all fours on wooden, sometimes metal, ladders. Their safety was only ensured by a rope tied around their waist, while their crampons, such as they were, lacked effectiveness because the leather straps weren't always well-tightened. On top of this, they also had to cope with the weather, wearing clothes that weren't really suitable for the freezing conditions.'

Gradually, the Sherpas established high camps that would allow Westerners to attack the summit. On 26 May, the British two-man team of Charles Evans and Tom Bourdillon failed in their attempt at the South Summit of Everest; their faulty oxygen system forcing them to turn back. The last team from the expedition to attempt the final ascent was that of New Zealander Edmund Hillary and the Sherpa, Tenzing Norgay.

On 29 May 1953, the weather conditions were perfect; the sun was shining and although it was almost –20°C (–4°F), the absence of any wind allowed the pair to progress quickly. Khamsu explained to his son that when he saw the summit, the New Zealander signaled to his companion to come alongside him so that the two of them could experience the monumental achievement together – an example of humanity that would bond the pair forever. As they reached 8,848 metres, Hillary took a photo of the Sherpa that would go down in history. In it, he poses, ice axe in hand, with the flags of Nepal, the United Kingdom, the United Nations and India, flying from its handle.

The two men did not stay up there for long, but there was enough time for Norgay to make an offering to the gods: a chocolate bar, some sweets, and some biscuits. Hillary, meanwhile, had taken off his oxygen mask for a moment and laid a small crucifix on the ground (as per the request of John Hunt, the British leader of the Everest expedition), which he then covered over with snow.

During their descent, the two men met George Lowe, a compatriot of Hillary's, who was waiting for them at the South Col with hot soup. George eagerly asked him, 'So? How was it up there?'

'Well, George,' Hillary replied, 'we knocked the bastard off!'

Tendi, who did not expect to hear such language from his father, burst out laughing when he heard this. Khamsu went on to explain to his son that Sherpas regard Sir Edmund Hillary as their "patron" because he showed tremendous generosity towards their community. At just 10 years old, Tendi became aware of the compassionate soul of his hero, who afterwards helped to build forty-two schools and hospitals in the Nepalese valleys.

Unfortunately, Sir Edmund Hillary died before Tendi could ever meet him. Yet from that moment on he had always dreamed of getting to know his descendants, and in 2018, he would finally cross paths with Hillary's son, Peter, in the Khumbu Valley. The New Zealander had already climbed Everest twice; in 1990, when he became the first son of a "pioneer" to reach the mythical summit and in 2002, this time with Jamling, the son of Tenzing Norgay. Peter told Tendi that he was getting ready to shoot a major film focussing on the third generation of the Hillary family, with the idea being to show the general public the evolution of climbing techniques since 1953. As well as this, the documentary would also chronicle the changing relationship between Sherpas and Westerners over the previous sixty-five years.

But the best was yet to come when Peter asked Tendi if he would play the role of Tenzing Norgay. Tendi could not believe it. What an honour! He would be filmed alongside Edmund Hillary's two grandsons, Alexander and George, who would be following in their grandfather's footsteps.

So in October 2019, Tendi finds himself in the Khumbu Valley, with a production team of ten people. The first scenes are shot with child monks, who are seen studying the sacred Tibetan texts, the images reflecting the few years that Tendi had also followed the Buddhist teachings. The Hillary brothers are in their twenties, and there is an immediate bond between the two young people and Tendi. For production reasons, as well for acclimatization, it is agreed that they will start by climbing Lobuche (6,145m) before continuing with Ama Dablam (6,812m). Filming takes a lot of time, as each action needs to be repeated up to ten times in order to achieve the best shots. Every day, Alexander and George strengthen their bond of friendship with Tendi, with George admitting that he would never have dreamed he would one day know how it felt to stand on top of the world, just like his grandfather had done in that historic first ascent.

'I was 16 when Ed died. I still remember his generous smile. He was a loving grandfather and definitely preferred talking about other people rather than telling his own "old stories" of his climbs. He was much prouder of what he'd achieved with the Sherpas than of talking about his glory as an explorer.'

Alexander also regretted not having questioned his grandfather enough about his exploits. However, he still had wonderful memories of playing hide-and-seek and building treehouses. To him, Ed was a grandfather just like everyone else's.

Tendi indulges the pair, telling them about his childhood in the remote region of Khembalung, followed by his long training to become a mountain guide. The two brothers instantly admire the Sherpa's incredible will, who was otherwise destined for a monastic life.

The ascent of Lobuche presents no major difficulties. Alexander and George have several expeditions to their credit, having already climbed Kilimanjaro, Elbrus and Mont Blanc, as well as exploring Antarctica, just like their father. Indeed, Peter's three children have always climbed with him, with his daughter, Lily, accompanying him to Everest base camp two years earlier.

So as to achieve a variety of shots, the film crew asks the mountaineers to reach the summit of Lobuche twice. As they do, a drone circles around them, revealing spectacular images. However, as the climbers wait at Camp 3 for them to set up the next shot, the cold and wind start to bite. Tendi starts to hop up and down to keep warm and launches into a Tibetan song. The two brothers quickly pick up the chorus as the three of them jump higher and higher. From a distance, it looks as if they are dancing to hard rock music, but the activity soon works its magic as they start to warm up again, and the wait seems much shorter than it did before.

The film aims to highlight the long preparation needed before facing Everest, so shooting continues on Ama Dablam, which stands at nearly 7,000 metres. It is a peak that Tendi reveres after climbing it alone following his very first ascent of Everest, and when they reach the summit, he takes the two brothers in his arms, filled with pride to be joined by the worthy descendants of Sir Edmund Hillary. With a broad smile on his face, George reveals that they are the first Hillarys to climb this particular mountain after their grandfather had led the first ascent in 1961, but had been unable to reach the summit. 'In 1979,' Alexander adds, 'our father attempted one of the most daring climbs of the time by going up the vertical, west face. Unfortunately, an ice avalanche put an end to his attempt at 6,300 metres. It was a miracle he survived.'

It was the grandfather of his new friends that paved the way for Tendi to be who he is today. Indeed, Sir Edmund Hillary empowered an entire generation of Sherpas to persevere in mountaineering, and Tendi feels overwhelmed with emotion whenever he thinks about it, even more so knowing that George and Alexander continue to hold the same beliefs as their grandfather.

The first stage of filming ends after forty-five days of trekking, climbing, ascending, interviewing and, above all, sharing their experiences. It is the director's hope that the following year, 2020, he will be able to film George, Alexander and Tendi in their ascent of Everest, with the aim of releasing the film on the 70th anniversary of their grandfather's historic exploit alongside Tenzing Norgay. Sadly, however, the project will fall through when the Coronavirus pandemic of 2020 forces the world to a standstill.

CHAPTER SEVEN

A PERFECT PYRAMID

TENDI SEES SWITZERLAND ALMOST AS a second home. He regularly finds himself dropping off his suitcases in the canton of Valais, usually staying with Armand, an old mountaineer who is like a father to him. In return, Armand loves the young man just as much as his own three children. Indeed, Tendi's fate would undoubtedly have been quite different had the pair never met. Armand supported and encouraged the teenaged Tendi in his dream of becoming a guide, providing him with wonderful opportunities to prove his motivation and skills, despite his young age. He also taught him French and funded much of his training.

It is a story that has linked their families for nearly two decades. Armand first befriended Tendi's uncle, Gyeljen, who quickly named him Saouji due to the fact that no one in Nepal could pronounce his first name. It is an affectionate nickname that actually means "boss", and since then, no one has called him anything else.

And so, each time Tendi comes to Switzerland, he tries to spend as much time he can with Saouji, despite the myriad of other invitations he receives. Unfortunately, as he never really has a fixed agenda, and finds it even harder to say 'no', he often ends up confusing his various appointments, much to the amusement of others. For example, one evening, the friends he was staying with had invited former expedition clients to join them, and while everyone was enjoying an aperitif, the doorbell rang. When Tendi opened the door, a charming young woman asked if he was ready to go; as agreed, she had organized a cocktail reception so his friends could see him again. With a slightly embarrassed smile, he finally left with her, leaving behind a large table without a master of ceremonies.

When in Switzerland, Tendi likes to take advantage of practising meditation with his friend, Nicolas Schneiter. The two men first met while Tendi was guiding his first expedition in his native valley. Surprised to learn that a Westerner practiced the same spiritual path as the Sherpas, Tendi gave Nicolas the nickname "Lama". For the past eighteen years, Nicolas has been pursuing this path, having received most of the Buddhist teachings; his clean-shaven head and a smile of rare generosity embodying all his kindness.

On this particular Wednesday, Tendi finds him outside Nicolas' chalet, a Nepalese flag floating on the terrace. After admiring the 4,000-metre mountains that rise in front of them, the two men go inside and position themselves cross-legged on yoga mats. With both hands in a prayer position in front of their chest, they greet each other before beginning the Buddhist prayer of Loving-kindness. Taking the prayer book dedicated to Chenrezig, Nicolas leads the meditation, beginning with the taking of Refuge. With their eyes closed and hands clasped, their bodies move back and forth in prayer as this first recitation allows them to connect with their deep spiritual nature. In front of them is a small booklet written in Sanskrit, with lyrics transcribed phonetically and then translated into French.

Pen tchir / sang gyé/ droup par sho//

May I attain enlightenment, for the benefit of all sentient beings.

Tendi continues with the Four Immeasurables, the "noble" attitudes towards all beings comprising of unconditional love, compassion, joy and equanimity. This is the moment to express one's wishes in order to achieve happiness and thus free oneself from suffering and its causes. Next, Tendi visualizes his father, Khamsu, on his right, and his mother, Dali, on his left, before imagining all the people he loves, as well as those he likes less, or who have made him suffer.

Although Tendi might not have mastered the philosophy as well as Nicolas, he still knows the sacred texts. During his meditation sessions with Tendi, which are all too rare, Nicolas feels in perfect harmony with this "soul brother", and together they share the same quest for inner peace. After various prayers and good wishes, they recite the fundamental mantra of Tibetan Buddhism, 'Om Mani Padme Hum'. They run their mala beads (a little pearl bracelet, similar to rosary beads) through their fingers, and pray to free all beings from their suffering.

Over an hour and a half later, Tendi turns on his cell phone. There are four missed calls and countless WhatsApp messages, each one an invitation to share a raclette (a Swiss cheese dish) or to meet for a friendly drink. A little overwhelmed, he reminds himself that he will not be able to accept all of them before his departure for Kathmandu, even though he hates to disappoint people. Instead, Lama advises him to call Saouji, who immediately comes up with a solution: why not gather all his Valais friends together in the same place and at the same time?

The party takes place three days later on a museum terrace in a small mountain village. Nicolas Bossard and Tendi arrive straight from the International Alpine Film Festival in Diablerets, where they have just received the public prize for 'Telenovela on Everest'. It is about 5.30 pm when the party gets going, with around fifty guests in attendance. Tendi is flattered that so many people have taken the trouble to come and tries to give everyone the time they need. As the majority of donors are present, it is also an opportunity for Tendi and Saouji to take stock of the latest work undertaken by their charity, Nepalko Sathi. The two men, supported by Khamsu, founded the NGO in the early 2000s with the aim of improving the living conditions of poor and remote areas of Nepal.

At 7 pm, Nicolas and Tendi wave goodbye to the guests and follow the road back to Zermatt. Two hours later, they pull two electric bikes out of Nicolas' van and in the dead of night, attack a dizzying climb through the forest, getting lost on their way and taking several detours. When the road becomes too steep for them to pedal any further, they dismount and continue on foot, finally reaching the Hörnli hut around midnight. The building sits at the foot of the north-eastern ridge of the Matterhorn, the mythical pyramid-shaped mountain famous throughout the world, particularly thanks to Toblerone chocolate!

Tendi and Nicolas roll out their sleeping bags on a rock. Surrounded by fresh snow and freezing temperatures, they manage to doze for a few hours before their set departure time of 4 am, just after that of the Zermatt guides and their customers. Tradition dictates that they have priority on the access road and although huge crowds are seen there in

August, today only about ten people are aiming to launch an assault on the summit. The spring weather has maintained a layer of snow and ice on the route, which is otherwise dry during the summer months, thus accounting for why there are fewer climbers in this particular season. However, although the weather forecast is good, a tenacious storm obscures the peaked summit.

Using only the light on their headlamps, Tendi and Nicolas jump from rock to rock, taking care not to cause any rockfalls that could threaten the mountaineers they have already passed along their way. Despite the difficult conditions, the men progress rapidly, but in front of them, at the end of fixed ropes screwed into the rock, another couple is moving at a much slower pace. By now it is already 10.30 am, and with the fog beginning to thicken and the wind starting to gust, the two men turn back without the slightest hesitation; even though the summit is only 100 metres away, they know full-well the dangers involved if they proceed. Ten people lose their lives on the Matterhorn every year, and they do not want to become part of the statistic. In the summer, the local helicopter company is called out regularly to rescue mountaineers, or worse, to evacuate the dead. Tendi and Nicolas even witness an accident on their descent when the woman they had passed earlier, who was struggling with her companion, suddenly slips on the icy rocks. They hear her scream but miraculously, the man manages to hold on to her. Wounded, she is later rescued by air.

At the end of the afternoon, the two men reach the hut where, ravenous, they devour a huge blueberry pie. Fascinated by Tendi's many exploits on Everest, the other clients and even the hut's caretaker ask him a thousand questions. A master storyteller, he apologizes for not speaking the haut-valaisan dialect and for more than an hour juggles between French and English. After a while, Nicolas points out to him that it is getting late, especially since they still have a long way to go, and so the two friends finally collect their electric bikes and head back to the van, reaching it in the early evening hours.

CHAPTER EIGHT

FIRST STEPS ON THE ROOF OF THE WORLD

BY THE EARLY 2000S, TENDI is almost 20 years old, and after years dreaming about climbing Everest's famous slopes, he is finally getting the chance. However, he will not be accompanying clients to the top, but instead will be going to pick up the huge amounts of rubbish left over from previous expeditions. Base camp itself is a dumping ground: tins, plastic bottles, broken crampons, tent pegs, gas and oxygen cylinders are piled up everywhere, and it gets not better the higher you climb.

The activity sparks the beginnings of a certain ecological awareness in the young Sherpa, who already has a great respect for the environment. It is also the opportunity to finally become part of the very closed circle of Everest workers. Nevertheless, the task is not without danger, but after measuring the risks, he believes he has the necessary skills. Arriving at the South Col (7,900m), he realizes that although he has never reached such an altitude before, his breathing, slow and deep, has a regularity that surprises him. Loaded with rubbish bags, and led by Ken Noguchi, a renowned Japanese mountaineer, the round trips between base camp and those at higher altitudes increases. To everyone's satisfaction, Tendi's team manage to bring back 8 tons of rubbish, including 400 empty oxygen cannisters. Tendi is delighted to have had such an experience, and with the enthusiasm of youth, he feels ready to accept any position going on the roof of the world.

His second expedition takes place on the Tibetan side. The ascent here is less dangerous than on the Nepalese side, but it is much more technical and the others assume that Tendi will not reach the top. What is more, his father has expressly asked him not to go above 8,300 metres due to his young age and lack of experience.

Fate, however, will decide otherwise, and when another Sherpa falls ill, the expedition leader asks Tendi to take over. This means he is now responsible for a client he knows absolutely nothing about. Yet in the famous death zone, it is imperative that the duo work closely together. At 45, Petko Totev is a former Bulgarian ski champion, but is still as fit as an Olympian.

Despite the fatigue and cold, the two men exchange a few words in their tent at Camp 4 (8,300m), before dozing for an hour or two and then eating their final real meal: freeze-dried spaghetti Bolognese. As they eat, Tendi remembers the advice his father gave him: 'You have to treat your clients as if they were children. When they're very tired, they often forget to eat and drink.'

They set off for the summit push at 10 pm, and because he has never been this high before, Tendi places all his trust in the fixed rope. The night is clear, with no wind. As his companion starts to show signs of fatigue, Tendi hands him some hot water and fruit juice. It is a tough climb for the young Sherpa, who, in addition to his personal belongings, also has to carry five bottles of oxygen. As they ascend, a strange nervousness starts to take over, accompanied by the feeling of being completely alone in the world. Suddenly, the light from his torch reveals a shocking sight: a corpse, frozen in the ice and snow. His Sherpa friends had warned him he would see things like this at the edge of the trail; the bodies of men and women who lose their lives every year en route to an unfinished dream. His stomach flips and he vomits bile, hastily wiping himself off with the lapel of his huge down jacket. As he takes a further step forward, the corpse plunges back into the deep night. Petko says nothing; he probably did not see it. The encounter makes Tendi wonder what life is about. Ashamed, he remembers that he has betrayed his parents' wishes, and blames himself for having disobeyed them.

At dawn, Tendi and his client reach the Second Step (8,610m); one of the difficult passages of the ascent. Up ahead, a ray of sunlight shines down on the summit ridge as if to welcome them. The walk is long and dizzying. Any misstep is fatal. After traversing another rocky passage, followed by a small ridge of snow, they finally arrive on the roof of the world.

With tears in their eyes, the two men, who a few hours earlier knew nothing of each other, share an emotional embrace. Tendi realizes that at this precise moment, no one on Earth is standing as high as them. He feels an immense pride to have brought so much happiness to his client, while at the same time humbled to have succeeded in his first summit of Everest, not to mention the fact that he was the one leading!

The following spring, setting off from the Nepalese side, Tendi joins an expedition made up of Austrians, Americans and Japanese, with the aim of transporting equipment to the higher camps. Each April, in extremely dangerous conditions, dozens of Sherpas mark out a route in the icefall in order to prepare a path that will later allow Westerners to take up their greatest challenge. They work for hours on this unstable mass, forced to slalom between the crevasses, securing dozens of steel ladders from edge to edge above the chasms.

Once the route has been established, Tendi's team begins to transport the equipment to the various camps. During warmer hours, serac (blocks or columns of glacial ice) falls are frequent, and it is for this reason that the round trips are usually made at night. The porters are aware of the dangers and always proceed with fear in their stomachs. Tendi is no exception, the young Sherpa at times having to imitate a tightrope walker in order to climb the ladders. Often assembled in two or even three parts, they oscillate slightly under his weight and make balancing very precarious, especially with the extra 30 kilos on his back and crampons on his feet. His safety is only ensured by two fixed ropes to which the climbers attach their carabiner. Further threats come from a hanging glacier at the Lho La Pass, and parts of it frequently collapse on the route. After heavy snowfall, avalanches can be triggered from the north face of Nuptse, making it impossible to find a safe route.

Tendi enjoys spending time at base camp and loves the atmosphere of this ephemeral city. He gets to know each group, making friends with the Western guides. The different medical emergencies fascinate him. He watches the doctors work as they treat frostbite, broken wrists and, most commonly, altitude sickness, taking note of all the actions that could potentially save lives. The other part of the camp that arouses his curiosity are the toilets. Waste management is overseen by the Pollution Control Committee, who remove the human waste on the backs of porters to a pit in Gorakshep, a small settlement located an hour's walk from base camp. When he was younger, his father had always told him that things like that were simply left on the mountain…

The bad weather persists for more than a week in this 2005 season. Several attempts end in failure and some of the groups give up completely, taking the decision to return to the valley below. A *sirdar* approaches Tendi to ask if he can accompany a Japanese client who still wants to climb as high as they can up Everest. The man in question, Keiichi Iwasaki, had left home four years ago without a penny in his pocket to cycle around Japan. Having completed this task, he decided he still needed another adventure and was now intending to complete a world tour, financing his journey by performing magic tricks along the way. Tendi cannot believe what he is hearing. The man has no experience of the mountains and even less of altitude. Arriving in Nepal, he had decided to go see what base camp looked like and, after a few days of mixing with the mountaineers, had an irresistible urge to climb Everest. None of the other expeditions clearly want anything to do with this beginner, but for Tendi, however, it presents a wonderful opportunity.

On 28 May the weather improves and Tendi leaves with this unusual client, intending to reach at least the South Col, which would be quite the achievement. Two days later, the men easily reach 8,000 metres and although the weather has so far remained fine, Tendi knows it can turn in an instant. Nevertheless, the cyclist feels fit and thoughts of attempting the summit start to form.

Tendi sets up the tent and lets his client rest, hooked up to an oxygen bottle. At this altitude, Sherpas are also obliged to use respiratory assistance so as to ensure the safety of others, and although Tendi does not really need it, he respects the rules. He melts snow for soup and tea over a tiny gas stove as the wind starts to pick up, buffeting the two-person tent with increasing ferocity. Despite the conditions, the two men set off at 8.30 pm for the summit push. The sky is clear, the moon bright, but the wind carries a great deal of snow, making the walk exhausting.

The ascent continues along unstable ground and, suddenly, he is faced with the same appalling sight as on the Tibetan side, when the light from his headlamp illuminates several bodies of mountaineers, frozen in the ice. To his credit, his Japanese client remains stoic. As he moves on, Tendi honours the memory of the unknown dead by reciting a prayer.

Upon reaching the Balcony, Tendi imposes a short stop to nibble on some dried fruit and change the oxygen bottles. The weather conditions remain poor as the two young men progress through the night like sleepwalkers, keeping a slow but steady pace. Tendi walks ahead with his head up, keeping sight of the razorblade-like summit ridge. To his left, a 2,400-metere abyss towards Nepal, to his right, a 3,000-metre void to Tibet. Staying focused is essential, but gradually the tiny path starts to widen.

As if by magic, the clouds suddenly disperse giving them the impression of floating on a tiny island. For Tendi and Keiichi, it would seem the planets have aligned, and at 8.30 am on 31 May, they reach the highest point in the world. The inexperienced man from Japan might as well have landed on the moon! After taking a few photographs, the next challenge is to get back down again safely. This is no easy task as they must once again traverse the same vertiginous ridge, while at the same time confront the other summiters who are arriving, in single file, along the narrow passage. As he surveys the route ahead, Tendi cannot help but think about how the scene resembles the traffic jams of mopeds on the streets of Kathmandu.

Keiichi is continuing his world tour even today, having never returned to his home country since leaving it in 2002. Still financing his travels thanks to his magic tricks, at the time of writing he is currently in Turin, Italy, preparing for his next project: rowing across the Atlantic Ocean.

CHAPTER NINE

NOT ONCE, BUT TWICE

IN 2007, AT 7,150 METRES ABOVE SEA LEVEL on the slopes of Everest, Brian Smith, an American client with the mountaineering company 'Mountain Madness', begins to have trouble breathing, even though he is lying in a tent in Camp 3. His respiratory rate is abnormally high. Not only that, he is also coughing up pink sputum, making him feel as if he is literally choking. Soon he starts fidgeting and showing signs of anxiety. Willie Benegas, the group leader, suspects he is suffering from a pulmonary edema. He explains to the Oregon real estate agent that his lungs are filling with fluid, hampering the passage of oxygen to his blood. A life-threatening emergency, cases such as this account for most altitude sickness-related deaths, and, if not treated quickly, Brian could slip into a coma and die within hours.

There is no other option: he must descend the mountain as soon as possible. Tendi and Ongdi, a fellow Sherpa, support him as they drop down 1,000 metres. After arriving at Camp 2, the American lies down in the tent and tries to get some sleep. However, at 2 am, he wakes up with a start, unable to breathe. As he passes in and out of consciousness, vomiting into his sleeping bag and alone in his tent, he realizes that he will die without immediate help.

Summoning a superhuman effort, he finally manages to get up. Before going out, however, he first needs to tie his shoes. The attempt lasts several long minutes, punctuated by nausea and discomfort. Having been unable to find his gloves anywhere, and even though it is –20°C (–4°F) outside, he crawls on all fours, with his bare hands in the snow. In the darkness, he does not know in which tent the two guides are sleeping. He shakes a first, no answer, then a second. With a rattling cry he shouts, 'Help! Help!' Panicked, Tendi and Ongdi emerge immediately, just as Brian collapses. He needs to be put on oxygen without delay, but in the middle of the night, it is impossible to find full bottles.

Without thinking about the dangers involved, in the dead of night, Tendi makes circuit of the camp to recover the remaining canisters. But more oxygen is not enough; Brian needs to lose even more altitude, and so at 5 am, the Sherpas make the choice to carry the American to base camp.

In "normal" circumstances, the journey across the Khumbu Glacier usually takes less than three hours. This time it takes them eight, crossing the formidable icefall in broad daylight, at maximum risk. When they finally reach base camp, Brian receives the help he needs. The doctor is amazed when he measures his saturation levels; at 61 percent, he is suffering from severe hypoxia and is in immediate danger of losing his life. After twenty-four hours of acute medical attention, the real estate agent is taken to Namche Bazar (3,400m), where he must regain his strength before being repatriated to Kathmandu.

Exhausted, Tendi and Ongdi rest for a few hours before returning to the upper camps. Tendi stumbles along the way, sprawling full length on the frozen snow. He gets up with difficulty, his face bleeding. Wracked with pain, the rest of the journey will be a genuine ordeal. The following night, Willie gives the go-ahead for the summit push, and Tendi prays to Buddha to give him the strength he needs. His prayers are clearly heard, as the 'Mountain Madness' team of Americans and Norwegians, led by the Argentinian Willie, easily make it to the summit.

During the descent, Tendi finds himself literally sleeping standing up. At the South Col, he slips into his tent and sleeps for nineteen hours straight. After another long rest at base camp, he calls his family. It is his mother, Dali, who answers the phone. Her son happily tells her the expedition was a success, but on the other end of the line, his mother's small voice sounds strange. She reveals that she is ill and that she needs to go to hospital to undergo a major operation. However, she then goes on to say that she will not be going because Khamsu, her husband, does not have enough money to pay for it. Tendi collapses, feeling as if he has been stabbed through the heart. There is no way he can sit idly by in the face of such a tragedy. Without hesitating, he assures her that she needs to have the operation; he will pay the bill. When she tells him the amount, however, he realizes that the money he is paid to be a porter will not be enough to cover it.

Meanwhile, Brian Smith, the real estate agent from Oregon who suffered a pulmonary edema, has recovered. The five days he spent at Namche Bazar has meant he is now in a stable condition and has decided it would be stupid to return to the United States without having made the summit. Everest has been his big dream ever since he was 15 years old – indeed, his 3-year-old son is even named after the famous mountain!

When questioned, the team doctor admits that to his knowledge, no mountaineer who has suffered from an edema has tried to reach the summit again in the same season. Brian asks him what his chances of succeeding are, only to be told that at barely 50/50, any such attempt would be sheer madness. To Brian, however, this answer is enough to satisfy him and so against medical opinion, the 37-year-old returns to base camp in a fighting spirit.

Willie Benegas studies his client's new health report and, persuaded by Brian's insistence, offers him the opportunity to try again, accompanied by his best Sherpa. Unsurprisingly, Tendi is the one chosen for the task. Taken a little aback by the request, Tendi asks his fellow summiters for their advice, only to be told that as far as they are concerned, his body will not be able to manage two successive ascents. Yet at the same time, he tells himself that the extra money is worth risking his life for to save his mother's.

Before reaching Camp 2, Brian, Tendi and Willie come across an expedition returning from Lhotse. Two men are carrying the body of Pemba, a Sherpani from Namche Bazar who had suffered a fatal fall while descending from Everest's neighbour. Tendi is upset; he knew the young woman well and wonders if by dint of taking risks, one day he, too, will end up like her. The gods have protected him until now, but how long will that last for?

It is the day of his mother's operation. Tendi is preoccupied, yet he needs to concentrate on his mission. The three men had planned to rest a little at Camp 4 before the final summit push, but one of their tents is destroyed by the wind and it is impossible for the three of them to fit in the other that survived. At around 9 pm, with a clear night and a bearable wind, they set off for the summit. In the final section, Brian recites the following mantra over and over to himself: 'I'm going to the top of the world. I'm going to the top of the world...'

At 2.50 am on 24 May, they finally reach the summit. Willie and Tendi move a few metres to one side, allowing Brian five minutes to himself as he stands there, completely alone, at the highest point on the planet. The thought enters the American's head that at that precise moment, nearly seven billion human beings are below him. It is also true that in the space of a week, Tendi has found himself on the summit of Everest not once, but twice. He takes no particular pride in the achievement. Instead, he thinks only of his mother.

By 6 am, they are back at the South Col. The Sherpas who are only just getting up are surprised to see the team heading back without reaching the top. When they learn the truth of what has happened from Willie, they can hardly believe their ears. No matter what, Tendi is a real hero. But despite the adulation, the young Sherpa calls home without any further ado to enquire about his mother. Fortunately, he is relieved to hear from his little sister, Lakpa, that the operation has gone well. Over 160 kilometres away, connected by the fragile line of a satellite phone, the brother and sister burst into tears as the emotion overwhelms them both. Fatigue quickly gives way to relief and Tendi feels truly blessed by the gods. Not only will his mother get better, but he will also return covered in glory with a nice bonus he can immediately hand over to Dali on her hospital bed. Before they part, Brian slips an envelope containing several hundred dollars into Tendi's hand; a well-deserved big tip. As the American pats him on the shoulder, he asks him, amused, if he is going to use the money to buy a computer or cover a Sherpani with jewels?

Much to Brian's surprise, his new friend's face suddenly turns serious, as he explains that the money is going to pay the surgeon who operated on his mother. Astonished, Brian realizes that at no point during the ascent did the Sherpa share any of his personal concerns. All his attention had been completely focused on his client. Ever since then, an unwavering friendship has bound the two mountaineering companions together.

CHAPTER TEN

AVALANCHES

IN 2009, AFTER COMPLETING SEVERAL Everest expeditions, Tendi is now looking forward to finally climbing Cho Oyu (8,188m). It is not just Tendi who is pleased; his family are just as happy because there are fewer dangers on this mountain than on Everest. However, as they are about to leave, his employer changes the programme. He is going back to Everest. That year, seven clients from a group led by the Benegas brothers succumb to the sirens of the world's highest mountain, so Tendi is hardly delighted with the thought of tackling it from the Nepalese side again. Nevertheless, he accepts his assignment, having confidence that his lucky star will continue to watch over him. He meditates in several monasteries on his way to base camp, hoping that the offerings he leaves will mean the monks think of him in their daily prayers.

Even before starting the climb, Tendi realizes he has lost weight and so must be vigilant; faced with such superhuman efforts, taking onboard the sufficient number of calories is essential. To protect the porters against the cold, the *sirdar* gives each of them an expedition jacket, clearly displaying the logo of a major brand. As he puts the jacket on, the young man thinks back to his father and how he worked on the slopes of Everest in his woolen clothes. At that time, not all porters benefitted from the same equipment as their bosses.

Before heading up to the altitude camps, Tendi calls his parents one last time. Khamsu knows full-well the dangers of the Khumbu Icefall on the way to the summit, but Tendi reassures his father that this season, the route is as safe as can be.

Leaving base camp, the formidable icefall appears at the heart of the Khumbu Glacier; a gigantic break in the slope that forms blocks of ice as tall and imposing as skyscrapers. This enormous structure, constantly in motion, begins to be dangerous as soon as the first rays of the sun appear. Consequently, most climbers cross the labyrinth before daybreak, but the crossing often drags on longer than intended. Multiple crevasses need to be crossed using ladders, which naturally takes a lot of time. So as the morning progresses, the risk of exposure increases.

Heavily loaded with equipment, Tendi and a young Sherpa called Phurba are in the middle of the icefall when an avalanche is suddenly triggered above them. Although small at first, it grows rapidly.

'Watch out! Avalanche!' goes the cry.

Other porters join in the shouting as they see the wave approach. Some drop their bags and run for shelter. Meanwhile, Tendi drags his friend under a serac and they hear a fierce rumble as a thick cloud of powder darkens the sky. The young Sherpa cries out, 'We're going to die! We're going to die!'

'Don't worry,' reassures Tendi, 'It won't get us.'

The cloud preceding the avalanche is already upon them, accompanied by a violent blast and rolling thunder. Tendi puts his arms around his companion's shoulders, protecting him with his body. Kneeling down in the snow, the white dust covers them completely.

'Don't worry, it's fine. Buddha will protect us. Everything will be OK!' Tendi says, soothingly.

Although he is trying desperately to calm Phurba down, inside, Tendi seriously thinks they are going to die. With his eyes closed, he says a prayer for his parents, brother and sister. Slowly, the intensity of the blast decreases, then stops. The ferocious din dies away, only to be replaced by the sound of Phurba coughing. The snow has invaded his airways but, after several minutes, his breathing starts to regulate and he comes to his senses. Tendi realizes that the avalanche itself has ended its journey in a deep crevasse; only the blast of wind that precedes the avalanche actually reached them. A miracle indeed.

Five years later, on 18 April 2014, Tendi comes face to face once again with a terrible avalanche. News of the event quickly spreads around the world, and the first press releases are particularly pessimistic, declaring, 'An avalanche that hit near Everest base camp has killed at least thirteen Nepalese guides. Three other people are missing.'

According to his schedule, Tendi was supposed to be in the exact spot where the tragedy struck. Hours pass and there is still no news. His friends are glued to his Facebook page, desperately waiting for any kind of sign from him. In Switzerland, people call Armand thinking he will have first-hand information, but this is not the case. The last message he received from Tendi was a week ago: 'Dear Saouji, my group and I are going to make offerings and receive advice from the *Lama* at the Tengboche Monastery. His blessings will protect us as we ascend. *Namaste* from Namche Bazar.'

Armand is sick with worry, while Khamsu and Dali are also without any news of their son. After a long, sleepless night, however, Saouji finally receives a reassuring phone call. Gobinda, the head of the local agency Tendi is working for, tells him that Tendi is alive. As soon as he has signal, he posts the following long-awaited message on his Facebook page:

'Hi everyone. I'm sorry to bring you bad news. We've lost our very best friends. I've been really busy with the rescues and recoveries of the bodies from yesterday morning and we have another long day today....'

It is another minor miracle that he was unharmed; clearly the *puja* that year had promised a fortuitous season. If Tendi had managed to escape the worst, it was only because forty-eight hours earlier, he had set off with his first cousin in the direction of Camp 2. Aged just 20, and only 1.50m (4'9) tall, little Tenji is still very inexperienced, but as a Sherpa needs to familiarize themselves with the high mountains, Tendi had decided to take him under his wing. He wanted to get him used to using crampons, as well as have the opportunity to acclimatize to the high altitudes. So, on 17 April, they had left at dawn and reached an altitude of 6,500 metres, before returning in the afternoon. During the descent, the temperature had increased significantly, and Tenji had started to feel tired, stopping frequently. Under the slopes of Lho La, Tendi realized that the situation was very precarious and urged his cousin to hurry back to base camp as quickly as possible. Without knowing it, they would end up spending a great deal of time in the same spot that would witness terrible tragedy only twenty-four hours later.

At around 7.30 am on 18 April, Tendi is still sleeping when a Sherpa, out of breath, tells him that an avalanche at

5,800 metres has just hit part of the base camp. Jumping out of his sleeping bag, he immediately tunes into the expedition's radio, but the only sound that comes out is an inaudible static. It is difficult to work out what has happened, but he quickly understands that there are several casualties, not to mention fatalities.

The Sherpas already at Camp 2 have rushed to the spot and after bringing aid to those injured, begin the search for the others. It is not long before they find their first victim, then several more. His ear glued to his radio, Tendi can hear crying and screaming in the background. His thoughts turn to his Uncle Angkaji. Loaded up like a mule in the middle of the Khumbu Glacier, the specialist had been equipping the normal route with fixed ropes, meaning if the avalanche had hit him, it would have been impossible to find any shelter. Despite several calls on his radio, no one answers, neither his uncle nor any other member of his group.

Tendi is the only guide in the camp to have solid experience in long-line rescue (using a long cable suspended from a helicopter winch). As the helicopter goes back and forth to the scene, more and more injured are returned to the camp. When they arrive, the doctors give first aid and triage the nine injured according to urgency. Three Sherpas are in a serious condition and are immediately evacuated to Kathmandu.

Once the wounded have been taken care of, it is now time to airlift the dead. The bodies are placed at Tendi's feet like disjointed puppets and, one after another, he picks up his friends. The last to arrive is indeed Angkaji, his mother's brother, and Tendi immediately thinks of his six cousins who will never see their father again. To make matters worse, Angkaji had been a single father after his wife had left him a few years earlier, leaving him to raise their six children alone. Another of the Sherpas who had lost his life was due to be married following his return from Everest. Concentrating on the macabre task in hand, Tendi does not even bother to wipe away the tears streaming down his cheeks. As a sign of respect, he touches the forehead of each dead person.

By 1 pm, rescuers are still trying to free a body with one foot protruding from the snow, but to no avail. Due to a persistent risk of further avalanches, all rescue attempts for that day must come to a halt. The next morning, 19 April, a group of porters and Western guides form a new rescue team. Two men are placed on sentry duty to sound the alarm in the event of a new avalanche. They manage to free the body found the day before, but three other Sherpas are still missing. Attempts at probe searches are unsuccessful, while all around them, scattered in the snow, the heaps of ice are soaked with the blood of the victims. Meanwhile, items such as battered bags, damaged helmets, shoes and torn clothes bear witness to the tragedy. Swept away by the avalanche while working on the ladders, it would seem the three men were thrown to the bottom of a crevasse 80 metres deep. All around him, the snow has become a shroud for Tendi's brothers.

Back at base camp, many of the Sherpas declare they do not want to proceed any further. In their view, it is indecent to walk on snow still red with blood. They have all lost friends and some, like Tendi, have lost family members. What has happened is a terrible tragedy, and for this close-knit community, recovering from such an event will be extremely difficult. Some group leaders, however, still want to continue, but as the tension mounts, three days later representatives from the Nepalese government arrive to calm things down.

Faced with threats from some of the Sherpas, one agency is the first to throw in the towel. Others soon follow, leading to the Nepalese state officially declaring the end of the season for that year.

Emotionally bruised, Tendi returns with his group to Kathmandu and spends the following days honouring the memory of the dead. He visits families and participates in cremation ceremonies, before finally going to the house of his late uncle. In tears, Chheji, Angkaji's eldest daughter, tells him that the orphans' pension they will receive will be no more than $400. Luckily, however, the company her father worked for had provided life insurance, meaning she will have an additional $15,000 on top of this. At 20 years old, she does not know if the sum will be enough to cover the needs of her five brothers and sisters. It leads Tendi to think about the other orphans of Everest; how will they be able to have a decent life? At present, he has no answer to this question.

A year later, in 2015, another avalanche will hit base camp, this time killing eighteen people and once again forcing the cancellation of the season. The avalanche itself will be caused by a huge earthquake, which in total will be responsible for the deaths of more than 17,000 people in Nepal.

CHAPTER ELEVEN

EARTHQUAKE

ON THEIR THIRD DAY OF ACCLIMATIZATION, Laly and Ulysse, Tendi's latest clients, are taking painkillers to combat their migraines, hoping they will pass quickly. After all, Everest is waiting for them! The advanced base camp on the Tibetan side is located 6,365 metres above sea level, and to get there the expedition has already had to travel along the "Miracle Highway", comprising of a 15-km moraine (soil and rock left behind by a glacier). It is worth it, however, with the long approach rewarded by a grandiose spectacle; the impressive, vertical façade of the highest mountain in the world.

It is 25 April 2015 and suddenly, in a fraction of a second, the earth begins to shake. The violence of the tremor takes everyone by surprise. There is general panic as some people are thrown to the ground, while others, panicked, run in all directions. Creaking ominously, the entire Rongbuk Glacier appears to be in motion. Huge avalanches career off the north ridge, threatening to hit the camp. When one stops, another is triggered immediately, each seeming even more gigantic than the previous. Luckily, the camp is safe; erected on a flat surface, it is far enough away from steep slopes and any potential dangers. After a few minutes, the earth stops shaking and a deathly silence sets in.

As the snow dust clears, Tendi realizes the magnitude of the drama. It is clear such a tremor must have been felt all over

Tibet and even beyond. Although his first thoughts naturally fly to his family (had the earthquake reached Kathmandu?), for now, at least, he has to take care of his clients. Fortunately, no one in the camp is injured and, after a quick appraisal, he grabs the satellite phone and tries to contact his family. Despite serious disruptions to the network, his father eventually picks up. The news from home is reassuring, even if, in the background, Tendi recognizes the crying of his 2-year-old daughter, Dolma. Khamsu has just enough time before the connection cuts off to tell him that their neighbourhood has been partially destroyed, and that in the capital, the dead are already being counted by the dozen.

The Chinese official in charge of chaperoning the climbers issues a demand via the radio that they withdraw to base camp, where their safety will be better assured. Tendi gathers his group together, knowing they must act quickly. As night begins to fall, the descent will only become longer and more difficult. Making their way back down, the path is illuminated by the light of a waxing gibbous moon, with only their headlamps providing an extra light source to help them see their feet. The long procession winds its way across the roof of the world, now more inhospitable than ever. It is not long before the aftershocks arrive, each one of them triggering yet more avalanches. In the icy night, the drum roll sound terrifies the mountaineers. They stop, clutching each other by the shoulders, clinging on to the noise of the mountain. When the din finally stops, they continue walking, not knowing if they will still be alive by daybreak. Setting the pace at the head of the group, Tendi focuses on his breathing, trying to rid himself of the stresses pulling at his stomach. Thinking of nothing except the present moment, he recites a series of mantras in an inaudible whisper.

After walking all through the night, the group finally reaches base camp, exhausted. The news they hear from the southern slope (on the Nepalese side) is bad; a gigantic avalanche has buried the other base camp. As usual, it was very busy at this time of the climbing window, and eighteen mountaineers have been killed, including friends of Tendi.

Fearing new aftershocks, the Tibet Mountaineering Association believes the mountain is no longer safe. However, despite the fact that several large crevasses have formed on the glacier, some expedition leaders insist on continuing. The majority of Sherpas, meanwhile, would prefer to be with their own; many of them still have no news of their families.

In the camp, discussions intensify as several of the clients still cling on to their hopes of being able to reach the top. Some of them have already had to give up their chances the previous year following the gigantic avalanche that hit the Nepalese side, which is one of the reasons they chose the Tibetan side this second time, as it is traditionally less exposed. They certainly do not want to have to give up their opportunity again if they can help it. After all, this is a lifelong dream for many, and a very expensive one at that.

As they wait for a final decision, Tendi decides to call his wife. Phuru explains to him that their house, which was built ten years previously, has managed to withstand the shock, no doubt thanks to the reinforced concrete foundations. In spite of this, Phuru says that they are still camping outside for fear of any upcoming aftershocks. The news makes Tendi want to cry. Stuck at the other end of the Himalayas, there is nothing he can do for his family, although the fact they are all still alive helps him focus on his role as group leader. Eventually, the Chinese government decides to halt any further ascents of Everest. Resistance is futile, and so the tourists and porters are sent to Lhasa, from where they can return to Nepal by plane.

The Air China Airbus is forced to circle Kathmandu for more than an hour before being allowed to land. Fifteen days have passed since the earthquake, and a nightmarish vision greets the passengers as they look out of the windows. The huge city has been gutted. Entire neighbourhoods destroyed. Crowds of people gather together in squares and parks, with the old houses in the Kopan district suffering particularly heavy damage. The taxi that takes Tendi home is forced to make huge detours to avoid the congested streets. People wander around, disoriented. Many of them are wearing bandages.

Tendi finds his family in the hastily set up makeshift camp. Their reunion is simple, but moving. He scoops up little Dolma in his arms, twirling her around in the air before putting her back on the ground, a moment of stolen happiness in the middle of such chaos. He takes his mother's hands. They bow to each other, forehead to forehead, then the same ritual is repeated with his father. Finally, he ends with a quick embrace with Phuru, his young wife.

A detailed inspection of the house reassures him that everything will be alright, and the decision is made to move back inside, although no one is exactly relaxed at the idea. The frequent aftershocks, even fairly light ones, can result in lasting mental health issues. At just 20 years old, Tendi's young cousin, Tenji, is having trouble sleeping, spending his nights, eyes wide open, staring into space. Meanwhile, Khamsu and his wife find solace in prayer, either in their private chapel or at the Boudhanath Stupa. Luckily, the temple remains usable, even though part of the monument has collapsed.

Tendi soon notices the lack of any form of coordination in Kathmandu: the police and army are seemingly absent from the city, while other logistical efforts to help are sorely lacking. NGOs are flooding the city in numbers, but, unfortunately, some of them are struggling to get up to operational speed quickly enough, leaving many of the earthquake's victims to fend for themselves in appallingly unsanitary conditions. Walking through the narrow streets of the capital is dangerous as entire sections of buildings are still collapsing all the time, with even Tendi only narrowly avoiding being hit by falling debris.

Khamsu is still desperately trying to reach Saisima, his home village, but communication in the isolated valley of Khembalung is still cut off. A friend tells him that a nearby hamlet has been completely flattened by a landslide, while the glacier that dominates the valley is threatening to collapse.

A former Argentinian client of Tendi's arrives to hand over a large sum of money, trusting him completely to make the best use of such a gift. So, with several 100-dollar bills in his pocket, he rushes out to buy a dozen large tents. Normally used as canteens during their expeditions, in a few hours, and with the assistance of several volunteers, the tents are erected in the heart of Naag Pokhari Park, near the Royal Palace. Thanks to this generous gift, 100 homeless people will no longer need to sleep on the streets.

At noon on 12 May, an aftershock of 7.3 magnitude causes further enormous damage, and even though their house once again manages to withstand the shock, a distraught Tendi and his family decide that it is much safe for them to leave the house and return to their camp outside.

Meanwhile, in Switzerland, Saouji is waiting for Tendi to clarify his priorities in terms of the aid needed. Just before calling him, however, Tendi posts the following message on Facebook:

> We had [a] terrible earthquake again today. We are forced to move out of home and we managed to set up the tents and we are sleeping in the tents rather than in our more comfortable rooms.

> My biggest concern is to all my friends all over Nepal, hope that they all are safe with their families and loved ones.

> With today's recent earthquake definitely many houses and building[s] have been destroyed and quite many loss of lives again.

> I have received lots of comments, Facebook messages and emails from all my best friends around the world, and it really helped us feel strong. We really appreciate all of your concerns and love and prayers.

At long last, Khamsu also manages to receive reassuring news from the Khembalung Valley. The damage caused there is minimal, apart from a landslide which has weakened the structure of the Saisima *gompa*. Tendi quickly relays the news to Saouji, while also telling him about the situation in a nearby Tamang village. Like the Sherpas, the Tamang are of Tibeto-Burman origin and share their Buddhist faith, meaning there is a close bond between the two ethnic groups. Moreover, some of the porters who work for Audantrek, the company Tendi and Saouji set up together, are Tamang. Most of the families in the village have lost parents, children or grandparents in the earthquake, not to mention their homes, food supplies and cooking equipment. A friend of theirs who runs the recruitment side of the company has already seen his wife and sister die in excruciating pain due to the fact that no help has reached them in over two weeks.

Saouji starts appealing for donations immediately, and Tendi's numerous Swiss friends quickly mobilize to raise $3,500, allowing him to travel straight to the stricken village. When he arrives, the reality goes way beyond what he had initially feared. The villagers who survived are in a state of great distress, having hastily been forced to cremate around twenty victims. Pyres are erected away from the rubble, and the bereaved members of the various families affected by the tragedy place their deceased on top. Surrounded by the glowing mounds, a *lama* recites mantras to unify the souls of each victim, which will otherwise remain in the bodies for weeks until the funeral feast can be organized, finally allowing them to leave and be reborn elsewhere.

For those left behind, the injured have had no first aid and have been left with little choice but to wait for help to arrive. Some of their wounds have become infected, while others have fractures that will now never properly heal. Their low food supplies are already exhausted, but a few days later, a truck chartered by Tendi and loaded with 8 tons of provisions finally reaches the village. Each family receives 30 kilos of rice and 3 kilos of lentils, which should be enough to keep them going until the situation improves.

Eight tons of rice, lentils and other foodstuffs are also delivered to Routbeshi, a small town north of the capital

Kathmandu. After distributing the food, Tendi and his friends improvise a delivery room in a large tent – a necessity given that there are around sixty pregnant women in the area with nowhere safe to give birth. What is more, the stresses brought on by the earthquake have already led to some women going into premature labour. However, the tent designated for the delivery room is sorely lacking in light, and so with the money given to him by his friend, Brian Smith, Tendi buys 100 headlamps identical to those used on their expeditions. They turn out to be ideal for the job as they provide good, localized lighting, while at the same time leaving the doctors' and midwives' hands free to assist the pregnant women. Finally, Tendi uses the remaining money from Brian to set up a dozen toilets in the surrounding disaster area.

Nepal, one of the poorest rural countries on the planet, was already relying on a heavily subsidized economy and charitable donations before the earthquake, but now even more people around the world are eager to help. Those charities already active in Nepal soon kick into gear, quickly followed by new organizations offering help. Unfortunately, however, with little knowledge of the country and even less of its customs, these newcomers are not as effective as their more experienced counterparts.

PART TWO

CHAPTER TWELVE

KHAMSU SHERPA

ROBUST DESPITE HIS SMALL SIZE, Khamsu has just turned 16. The young Sherpa lives with his family in the isolated region of Khembalung, a huge glacial valley in eastern Nepal, where he helps his parents cultivate the land and shape new terraces. Like a lot of Nepalese men, he also works as a porter. After all, carrying goods on one's back up and down these narrow, steep paths is the accepted way to transport most cargo. He carries down potatoes and kodo millet (a grain common in Nepal and a staple diet of Nepalese highlanders) to Rai villages, bringing back rice, salt, and other useful agricultural and household items on his return. At 16, he can already carry more than 30 kilos, but his pride as a young Sherpa always pushes him to increase his load, particularly when he goes looking for wood in the jungle or stones from the river. In the summer of 1976, he helps to tend the herds in Saisima, his village, but meanwhile plans to become the local *lama*, just like his father and uncle before him. Encouraged by his parents, he studies at the monasteries to learn the different mantras, even though he secretly also harbours dreams of going out and discovering the world.

Several Sherpas from nearby Gonthala have signed up as expedition porters, which will allow them to bring home a small salary. Khamsu's village is dominated by Makalu which, at 8,485 metres, is the fifth highest mountain in the world. The summit is coveted by many Western mountaineers and the path leading to the base camp has become a popular trekking route. Khamsu can clearly see his opportunity of finding work, but unfortunately, he knows nothing about the role and what it involves. On his friends' advice, he travels to Tashi Gaon, the last village on the way to the summit, where the Rai porters who were employed in Hile refuse to proceed any further up the mountain as they do not like the high altitudes. The opportunity could not be more perfect.

He leaves Saisima at dawn. Barefoot and wearing the only clothes he owns (the traditional dress of Sherpas and Tibetans), his felted woolen coat is open at the front and reaches down to his knees. The two sides cross at the chest, secured at the waist by a belt. He packs some food for the journey in a small canvas bag, including *tsampa* (a Tibetan staple made from roasted barley flour mixed with milk or tea) and potatoes cooked in their jackets. A round knitted woolen cap covers his head and attached to his belt is his kukuri machete, which will be essential for clearing a path through the jungle or for defending himself against wild animals. Finally, a woolen blanket, folded over his shoulder, completes his outfit.

As he runs down to the bottom of the valley, he finds the rarely travelled path overgrown with vegetation. Nevertheless, Khamsu is accustomed to walking quickly and continues briskly through the jungle. Arriving at the ridge, his gaze turns towards the horizon. To the north stands Chamlang (7,319m), at the foot of which he has grazed yaks for several summers. The peak forms part of the sacred mountains that protect his village and is connected to the sharp edges of Makalu, which itself represents the hope of earning his own living.

The sun is still high in the sky when he sees the first houses of Tashi Gaon, and he sets out to find out where Dolma, a girl from Khembalung who has recently married a Sherpa from the village, lives. Sherpas are naturally hospitable and with hands stretched forwards in the traditional Sherpa greeting, he is warmly welcomed with cries of '*Tachidélé, tachidélé!*' The butter tea and *tsampa* he is given help to relieve the hunger twisting his stomach, as Norbu, Dolma's husband, arrives from the fields and is as welcoming as his wife.

Khamsu soon learns that part of Norbu's business is serving foreign tourists, and that a group are due to arrive a couple of days to head up to the Makalu base camp. Having never seen any foreigners before, he has no idea what these people will look like or how they will behave. Norbu tells him that they are strange people, who wash themselves several times a day, sit on chairs to eat and, even more surprisingly, wipe their behinds with paper. Khamsu cannot believe his ears but knows that his friend is teaching him as many things as possible so that he is not too shocked during his first contact with them.

Norbu promises to speak with the *sirdar* on Khamsu's behalf but cannot guarantee anything, as there are already dozens of young people waiting for the caravan to arrive in the hope of being hired as porters. Pasang, Norbu's cousin, is responsible for choosing the location of the camp and organizing its layout. He lays out some markers while explaining to Khamsu, 'This shelter, at the edge of the field, will be used for the kitchen, with another tent serving as a dining room erected nearby. The tourists' tents will be aligned, facing the valley, so that they can enjoy the scenery.' Khamsu listens, intently, imaging himself helping out as one of the kitchen boys.

In the afternoon, two porters carrying the tents arrive, followed by another four carrying the Westerners' personal belongings. The volume of stuff takes Khamsu by surprise. How many tourists must there be to constitute so much luggage?! He is told there are eight of them in total, with two people per tent, and that everyone already has their own backpack with them, in addition to what has been brought on ahead.

'*Kuire ayo! Kuire ayo!*' chant the barefoot children. 'The tourists are coming!'

Dressed like his clients, the *sirdar* walks at the head of the column. Clearly unused to such steep terrain, he remains attentive to the tourists as he tries to keep them to the same tempo used by the inhabitants of the high mountains. Under the cook's direction, the kitchen boys spread out utensils and food on tarpaulins, the sheer quantity and variety of goods on offer never failing to amaze Khamsu. When the climbers finally arrive at the camp, the young man suddenly realizes that he has never seen white people before. He observes them, discreetly, as the kitchen boys assemble two tables and eight chairs. Water is boiled for tea, and biscuits are laid out on a plate. All the while the porters have a terrible time trying to keep the curious village children at bay as they crowd around the camp. Over to the side, the *sirdar* pays those porters who have decided not to continue any further. Unsuitably dressed, these Rai porters cannot abide the cold and will leave that same evening for less demanding altitudes.

Sitting upstream from the camp, cross-legged, Khamsu continues to observe, intrigued. Before this, his world has been limited to the villages of his valley. When he was a child, his father explained to him that behind the mountains of Saisima lay Tibet. He would sometimes see caravans coming from the

In spring 2022, Tendi completed his twentieth season on Everest. © Pasang Sherpa

The Base Camp establishes its spring quarters on the immense Khumbu Glacier. © CTSS

A VIP tent at Everest base camp, 5,365m. © CTSS

Crossing the Khumbu Icefall marks a precarious moment in the ascent of Everest. Before each season, about ten 'icefall doctors' equip this section of the Khumbu Glacier with ladders and handrails. As you would expect, working on a constantly moving mass of seracs and crevasses is dangerous work. © CTSS

The summit ridge is the narrowest passage of the climb. © CTSS

The puja is a ceremony where the mountaineers ask the gods for permission to climb the Himalayan mountains. © CTSS

In Nepal, it is common for children to undergo religious training. Tendi was no exception and spent five years learning Buddhist teachings at his village school. © Ivan Hughes

Tendi and his client, the Argentine actor Facundo Arana, during their ascent of Everest from the Tibetan side in 2016. The weather can still be warm, even at 7,200m! © Nicolas Bossard

George and Alexander Hillary, the grandsons of Sir Edmund Hillary, approaching the high camp on Labouche with Tendi in 2019. © Nyamgal Sherpa

Inauguration of the Naya Saisima Community Center, founded by the Tendi Sherpa Foundation.
© Author's collection

The house where Tendi was born in
the remote village of Saisima.
© Hilary Sutherland

©Nepalko Sathi-Amis du Népal

A community garden project
in the villages along the
Khembalung Valley.
© Nepalko Sathi-Amis du Népal

Tendi, his wife Furwa, and their daughters, Dolma and Dechen, in traditional Sherpa dress.

© Author's collection

Tendi looks on Saouji as his own father, and it was Saouji who taught Tendi how to use a map and compass on his first visit to Switzerland in 2004. © Author's collection

Practising rescue techniques with Swiss rescuers. © Author's collection

Skiing is a new sport for Tendi, who likes to practise it in
Switzerland, or here in Aspen, Colorado. © Dave Schaeffer

Antarctic expedition, 2021. © CTSS

The closing disco at the end of the First Aid training week in La Fouly, Switzerland, winter 2016.
© François Mathey

The legendary Matterhorn, Switzerland. In 2021, Tendi failed to reach its peak by the barest of margins.
© Author's collection

Lakpa and her husband, Pasang. An excellent mountain guide, Pasang often accompanies Tendi on his expeditions. © Author's collection

Tendi with his daughters, Dechen (left) and Dolma, after returning from Everest. © Author's collection

Tendi with his parents, Khamsu and Dali, his wife Furwa, and daughter Dolma at a Sherpa party. © Author's collection

Olya Lapina practising her daily yoga at Manaslu's Camp 4, 2014. © Kuntal Joisher

Tendi and Mike Hamill meticulously study the weather forecasts before kicking off their Everest summit bid. © Magda Lassota

At the summit of Mount Vinson, Antarctica, Christmas 2021. © Author's collection

Tendi took this photograph of Everest before sunrise during his ascent of Lhotse with Gabby Kanizay.

© Author's collection

Gabby Kanzinay, 19, and her mother Jane at the summit of Everest on 14 May 2022. © Author's collection

Tendi on Everest for the fourteenth time in his career. © Lakpa Sherpa

A tribute to Tendi's North American client who died on the slopes of Manaslu. © Lakpa Sherpa

country and was surprised by the fact the travellers spoke a language close to his own. In reality, it was the language of mantras, the ones he himself practiced.

The *sirdar* pulls him out of his thoughts, beckoning him to come over. He stares at him with a haughty expression as Khamsu looks down, intimidated.

'What ethnicity are you? Have you ever worked for a trekking agency?' the *sirdar* asks.

Khamsu confesses his inexperience but assures him that he can walk quickly and for a long time, even when carrying a heavy load on his back. Luckily, the *sirdar*'s face softens, 'You might make a decent kitchen boy. I'll give you 300 rupees [$2.50] a day. You can eat in the kitchen but be warned; if you don't work to my satisfaction, I'll send you back immediately.'

CHAPTER THIRTEEN

SERVING THE WESTERNERS

NORBU TAKES KHAMSU TO THE kitchen tent, where a small tubby man is hard at work.

'Here's your new kitchen boy,' he says. 'Good luck. He's got a lot to learn!'

Pemba, the cook, takes him by the hand and looks at him up and down.

'The first two things you must learn are to wash your hands and don't spit in the camp. You need to break these bad habits. You must always be as polite with the tourists as you are with the *lama* of your village. Dawa will help with your training.'

At that, a young man crouching nearby, cleaning an alcohol stove, turns towards Khamsu.

'There's no time for fun here. Go fetch some water with Dorje – you have to make sure it never runs out!'

Dorje is a tall, slim teenager, the complete opposite of Khamsu. He hands him two empty jerry cans and leads him over to a stream where they fill the 20-litre containers at a small waterfall.

'Make sure you wash your hands well if you don't want to be yelled at by Pemba,' advises Dorje. 'You'll soon learn how he makes himself heard when he's unhappy, but apart from that, he's nice and gives us good food. Generally, we tend to prepare too much food for the *kuires* [the name given by the Nepalese to foreign tourists]; that way, there'll always be something left over for us.'

When they return, Dawa, still squatting, is peeling cooked potatoes. Khamsu kneels down beside him and gets to work. His new colleagues are Sherpas, like him, so they should get along well. Pemba cuts up a chicken, but as a good Buddhist, Khamsu has never eaten meat before. After all, how can you kill an animal just to eat it? It sickens him to know tourists eat meat almost every day. These people have no respect for religion, he tells himself. The Rais are also carnivorous, and are often reproached by the Sherpa people for not having gods.

As night falls, everyone fears Khamsu will make a fool of himself in front of the clients, so he is kept away. Plates, knives, spoons and forks are laid on the cloth-covered tables. Back home, Khamsu and his family eat with their fingers from a communal pot. As the food is brought to the canteen tent, the *kuires* take up their spoons and tuck into the soup. Next comes a chicken curry, accompanied by sautéed potatoes and a dish of raw vegetables. Finally, canned fruit is brought out for dessert. Khamsu has never seen such an abundance of food, and as soon as the meal is over, the three kitchen boys run to the river to wash the dishes in the frozen water. It takes a great deal of vigorous scrubbing to remove all the grease. Meanwhile, at the edge of the forest, the other porters light a fire to heat the leftovers. Khamsu ignores the meat, naturally.

That night, wrapped in a blanket in a corner of the kitchen, Khamsu searches in vain for sleep, too worked up by his first day. It is still dark the next morning when the cook shakes him awake and gives him his first orders. Breakfast is eaten at sunrise and everything must be ready on time. Khamsu looks at the two petrol stoves as they emit a steady hum. The equipment is foreign to him, but it certainly seems more practical than going to look for wood in the jungle. He prepares the dough for the *chapatis* (unleavened flatbread) and as he does his thoughts turn to his mother, who makes them wonderfully.

The tourists wake up at 7 am sharp. 'Tea time,' whispers Dawa, squatting in front of the first tent. No answer. 'Tea time,' he says again, a little louder. Khamsu hears the noise of a zipper followed by the appearance of a disheveled head of light brown hair and stubble through the crack of the tent. Khamsu is struck by the man's blue eyes; he has never seen anything like them before.

'Sugar? Milk?'

Crouching down, Dawa adds a spoonful of sugar and presents the cup with both hands, maintaining his bow all the while in the traditional Nepalese way. The gesture of offering something is important and never done so lightly, and as a second cup is served to the disheveled man's companion, they move on to the next tent. It is the first direct contact Khamsu has had with foreigners. After tea, the two Sherpas bring a bowl of water to each person for washing. One man washes outside, completely naked, and although he is only visible from behind, Khamsu is outraged by such shamelessness.

The dining table is set up outdoors and features cereals with milk, potatoes, *chapatis*, butter, jam, and coffee, a drink Khamsu is, as yet, unfamiliar with. Dressed and kitted out for departure, the tourists have already packed their big bags and so the porters load them on their backs and set off. For acclimatization reasons, and to help limit headaches, the next stage will be short. Everyone will head straight to the next camp so there will be no need to stop for lunch, and while the Westerners are used to having their main meal at midday, the Sherpas are quite used to heading out to the fields on an empty stomach, usually returning around 10 am for their main meal, which is often the only meal of the day.

In the hubbub of the departure, the kitchen team finish the dishes. They are the last ones to leave and have to walk very quickly if they are to arrive at the next camp before the trekkers. Nevertheless, despite a steep climb and the weight of their packs, they soon overtake the Westerners, setting up the camp by the middle of the afternoon. Khamsu is intrigued by a narrow, high tent erected away from the main camp: the toilets. Would it not just be easier to go and relieve yourself in the great outdoors? But Dawa explains to him that this way of doing things is much more hygienic; the hole for the excrement will be filled with earth when they leave, leaving no trace behind.

CHAPTER FOURTEEN

YOUNG EMOTIONS

DESPITE THE ALTITUDE, IT IS STILL pleasantly warm at the camp and so when the cook allows him a bit of time off until teatime, Khamsu decides to take a stroll. Sitting cross-legged on a flat stone, his eyes scan the high pastures where he spent his childhood herding yaks. Above him, the enormous icy mass of Chamlang stands out against the fire-coloured sky. He can make out the crenellated ridge of his village's sacred mountain, home to the gods who watch over the people below.

The environment is perfect for meditation and so Khamsu begins to recite the mantras, even though his thoughts keep returning to the tourists with their strange customs. His attention is soon drawn to a young woman whose light, very low-cut garment reveals the roundness of her breasts. Sherpa girls always dress so as to reveal nothing of their anatomy underneath, and although he initially takes offense at her behaviour, he cannot help but feel a certain excitement at the same time, as a soft heat rises along the nape of his neck. The young woman has an oval face with a light, pale complexion, which he finds much more beautiful than the wide, dark Sherpanis. With her blond hair falling over her shoulders and her clear gaze, she looks every bit the goddess. Indeed, Dawa calls her *Sunderi Keti*, the pretty girl.

As the Sherpas find it hard to pronounce and even remember the Westerners' names, they instead give them nicknames related to their appearance or behaviour. So, the man who shares the pretty girl's tent is called *Zungue*, the bearded one. For the older couple in the group, it is simply *Baze* and *Bazu*, grandfather and grandmother. The group's leader is a regular in Nepal and speaks a few words of Nepali. He shares a tent with *Tablé*, the bald one. One woman, thought to be a bit haughty and arrogant, is quickly nicknamed *Gamandi*, the proud. Her tent companion, with a smile everyone loves, is *Hansne Bouri*, the laughing woman.

The nicknames soon make it easy for Khamsu to recognize each member of the group, even though he still dare not approach them or meet their gaze. He finds himself feeling ashamed of what he is; a small mountain peasant who knows nothing of the world and a figure of great interest and wonder for the Westerners. He is soon conscious of the poor quality of his clothes, wishing he could wear beautiful garments like the *sirdar*. Even those worn by his fellow kitchen boys are in a better condition than his.

The tourists' incomprehensible language seems garbled, devoid of those harsh sounds which make the Sherpa language so charming. He wonders how these rich people see him. Do they despise him? Gamandi almost certainly does, but Sunderi Keti looks kind so she must be different. Could such a woman possibly marry a Sherpa, he wonders, before quickly pushing the incongruous idea out of his mind.

The next day's stage is also very short and although the location of the camp is good, it is half an hour's walk to find water. With a little dread, Khamsu quickly realizes that from here on in, the paths and surrounding ground are all covered with snow, and he knows how painful it is to walk barefoot in such conditions. Fortunately, that afternoon the *sirdar* hands out Chinese army sneakers to all the porters. They are not very warm, but at least they are preferable to having bare feet. The other porters have socks, but Khamsu has never owned a pair. In fact, at 16, he has never even worn shoes before and when he tries them on, the sensation of feeling as if his feet are being squashed is extremely unpleasant.

The temperature drops sharply after sunset and the Westerners rush to put on their down jackets. Khamsu considers how much more comfortable they must be than the woven wool coat he has on. Wrapped up in his blanket, however, he finally enjoys a good night's sleep; the three kitchen boys and cook huddled together, the better to resist the cold.

When the time comes to depart the next day, the sun has crossed the ridge line and the air has warmed up considerably. Perturbed by his sneakers, Khamsu dreads slipping on the frozen ground, but soon gets used to walking in them. Lunch is taken near a small lake with dark waters and as the tourists linger for a while, Khamsu longs to do the same. A divine spirit seems to emanate from the place, perfect for meditation.

That evening Hansne Bouri approaches him while he is bringing water supplies back to the camp. With a broad smile, she hands him a pair of thick socks. Confused, he does not know if he should accept, but the woman insists and he ends up taking them with both hands, bowing respectfully. Hansne Bouri smiles, maternally caressing his cheek with her hand. Surprised by the gesture, Khamsu blushes and quickly leaves her to return to the camp.

The next midday meal is taken on an alluvium deposit (loose clay, silt, sand, or gravel left behind by running water in a stream bed or on a floodplain etc). As the sun enters the gorge, the temperature finally becomes pleasant. When the trekkers arrive, Khamsu hastens to offer them tea. Hansne Bouri comes up to speak to him, but he cannot understand what she says. She points to herself saying, 'Mary... and you?'

He presumes she is asking him his name.

'Khamsu Sherpa', he mumbles, shyly.

'Khamsu... Khamsu...' repeats the woman, trying to memorize it.

Unable to understand why the woman would be interested in him, Khamsu carries on serving the others, his head down, embarrassed.

Every day the behaviour of the foreigners presents many new surprises for him. On one occasion, on his way to fetch water from the river, he surprises a young couple kissing. Sherpas would never be seen in such an act, but although Khamsu is shocked, he is also suddenly overwhelmed with impure thoughts, picturing himself embracing this young woman, beautiful as a goddess.

The next day, heavy clouds cling to the mountains and shroud the sun. Served outdoors in the freezing cold, mealtime is hardly pleasant. Khamsu is used to the cold and so tries to ignore it, but he cannot wait to get back on the road again. As they arrive at the next camp, the tourists shut themselves in their tents, only coming out to go to the canteen.

The expedition finally reaches Makalu base camp and the trekkers are allowed to rest the following day. It is also a welcome opportunity for the kitchen team, who so far have had no respite on the journey up the mountain. On their day off, the youngest tourists decide to set out on an all-day excursion, with only Gamandi and Hansne Bouri preferring to stay behind and rest. Always agreeable, the latter moves closer to the kitchen boys and tries to communicate with them. With a smattering of English, Dorje is able to answer some of her questions, leaving Khamsu to sit there silently, daydreaming. How is it that she can be here, without her husband or children, he wonders? It is not normal. She looks at him with a genuine tenderness. Perhaps she is the reincarnation of Dolma, Buddha's mother?

The journey back is a real pleasure and as the route is essentially downhill, it allows the 16-year-old Khamsu to run a good part of the way. Now that most of the food reserves have been eaten, the packs he carries are much lighter. Exchanges with the Westerners are more frequent, and Khamsu has the impression that everyone likes him. Now that the expedition is coming to an end, he starts to think about the 4,500 rupees he has earned – more money than he has ever possessed or even seen before! He bids farewell to tourists, who are generous with their tips. Hansne Buri offers him a pair of trousers that are slightly too long, but if he rolls them up then they will fit perfectly. As he prepares to say goodbye to his benefactress, Khamsu takes both her hands and presses them against his forehead, bowing as he does so in total respect. The woman pulls him up, hugs him to her body and kisses him on the cheek. As far as he can remember, no one has ever shown him such tenderness before, not even his mother. It is a very moving experience.

During the expedition, Khamsu has learned that a smart boy can quickly climb the ranks and become *sirdar*. Others, meanwhile, are destined to remain porters and end up old before their time, their bodies marked for life by the harsh conditions. However, he also realizes that without mastering English, it will be much more difficult for him to progress.

Meanwhile, one of the other porters tells him that he is going to go build houses in Sikkim. Hired by a merchant from

Khandbari, it is a sector that provides a great opportunity to earn a lot of money. Tempted by the prospect, Khamsu leaves with a contract in hand. In the years to come, no one will really know what happened to him during those two years he worked in Sikkim. He would never speak of it. Back in his home village, however, everyone guesses that it must have been the saddest period of his life; a life as a slave. To make matters worse, during his time there he would be robbed of the money he had hoped to bring back, leading to a shameful, disappointed and penniless Khamsu who would eventually return to his family.

CHAPTER FIFTEEN

ARRANGED MARRIAGE

KHAMSU HAS BEEN PROMISED TO Dali, a young girl from the Goperma tribe of Gonthala. The marriage has been arranged by their parents and even though the young girl is very beautiful, and he likes her a great deal, Khamsu still believes he is not mature enough for such a big step. A stubborn young man, he resists the decision, determined that no argument can make him change his mind. He manages to convince his father to send him to Kathmandu so that he can earn more money by working for the trekking expeditions. Surely the wedding can wait?

It is the end of the monsoon season and his cousin from Gonthala, who is working as a *sirdar* with a big agency, has promised him three successive expeditions. His salary will be 400 rupees ($3.50) a day for two months. A good start. If he proves himself, however, he is told he'll be able to join an expedition to Everest the following spring. Although trekking on the icefall is dangerous work, he knows the payoff will be worth it.

Fortunately, his skills are soon recognized, and, within a few seasons, he is given more and more interesting assignments. Unfortunately, his ascent up the porter hierarchy is limited by his lack of education and poor command of English. But, as he says to himself, *Ké garné*? What can you do?

During one expedition, Khamsu is asked to lead a team of porters to Upper Dolpo, while the client tourists are flown directly to Jumla, accompanied by their *sirdar*. The monsoon has not quite finished with them yet, however. It rains several hours a day, making the paths muddy and difficult to navigate, and meaning the porters' clothes are permanently wet. Even worse, it would appear the *sirdar* has not planned ahead well enough and after three days of walking, the food is starting to run out. The Nepalese are furious and hold Khamsu responsible, even threatening to strike. When they arrive in Jumla, the *sirdar* even accuses him of having resold the food. During the rest of the expedition, the quarrels will severely tarnish the atmosphere, and for Khamsu, who always appreciates friendship and conviviality, the accusation is unbearable.

On another expedition, Khamsu finds himself clinging to the fixed rope on Makalu's steep slopes. He is just under 5,000 metres above sea level, caught in the eye of a fierce storm. Once they reach base camp, the small group of porters spend the night outside, huddled against each other, shivering, with only a tarpaulin for protection. Ten metres away, in a furnished canteen, the *kuires* eat hot soup and laugh out loud, wrapped up in their big down jackets. Once the climbers have finished their meal, the Nepalese are allowed to share the leftover food and barricade themselves in the communal tent.

During this particular trip, carried out at the beginning of the 1980s, the porters are given no extra clothing and have to content themselves with their own outfits, which are completely unsuitable for the high altitude. Indeed, during an expedition to Dhaulagiri (the seventh highest mountain in the world at 8,167m), Khamsu sees a fellow Sherpa die from cold and exhaustion. At the time, foreigners had the power to charge locals particularly low rates, caring little about the impact on staff and the risks involved. Now, nearly forty years later, the former *sirdar* is proud of what his son is doing to improve the porters' working conditions, be they summiters or simple porters, and is pleased that this new generation of international guides, including Tendi, are imposing a strict working ethos on this tourism industry.

After each trek period, Khamsu returns to his village. His mother relies on him to go down to the lower valley for supplies, and, on the way, he is obliged to stop at the family home of Dali, his future bride. At first, Khamsu is rather sulky, ignoring the girl his parents have chosen for him as he speaks with her father by the fire. Dali automatically keeps away at first, but over the coming weeks, the young people get closer with each visit. She waits for him, away from the house, and the few secretive, tender gestures they share begin to awaken deeper feelings in Khamsu. Deciding that they have waited long enough, their parents announce their engagement. Khamsu still does not feel ready yet, however, and is already looking forward to going on another expedition. Nevertheless, he promises to submit to his parents' will on his return.

On Everest, Khamsu works as a high-altitude porter, going back and forth numerous times between base camp and the South Col. He hates crossing the icefall, constantly praying that nothing will happen to him. Any free time he has, which is rare, is devoted to prayer and meditation. He also begins to think more tenderly of Dali, with visions of his future bride often taking precedence over his prayers.

On his return he decides to buy her a necklace of turquoise stones from Tibet. He feels almost carried away by love and practically runs the final section towards Gonthala. The family is hastily reunited in the village, and the *chang* (Tibetan barley wine) flows freely. Drinking more than he probably should, Khamsu loves its fermented taste as it burns his throat. Drunk with alcohol and fatigue, Dali leads him onto a mat, out of sight, and for the first time in his life, he finds himself snuggled up against the body of a woman. A woman who would from henceforth be his wife.

The young couple spend a year living with Dali's parents, before moving in with Khamsu's family in Saisima after the wedding, where life immediately becomes more difficult. There are too many people in such a small space, so the young husband decides to build his own house. In the meantime, he erects a makeshift shelter to give them a basic amount of privacy during the few months the construction will last. Sadly, what was supposed to be temporary seems to go on forever, and as months quickly turn into years, the hut moves from being particularly humid during the monsoon season, to freezing cold during the winter.

Each trekking season, Dali has to come to terms with the fact that Khamsu disappears. Between looking after the livestock, growing crops, and preparing meals, the young woman must also collect the stones needed for the house and transport them to the building site. The biggest stones are broken in situ in order to create more transportable pieces, after which they are cut so as to form rubble that can be used for building the walls. Meanwhile, the unwanted bits are broken down into a fine powder to be used as mortar; there is no cement here in the depths of Nepal.

Dali's belly soon begins to grow, and it will not be long now before their first child is born. Over the weeks, the work becomes more and more difficult, only increasing her anxiety.

Each birth is source of genuine happiness, but in the land of the Sherpas, childbirth can often end in disaster. There are no doctors or midwives nearby, and as the people of Saisima are more used to looking after cattle, they treat human births in the same manner. If any misfortune occurs, it is undoubtedly the will of the gods.

In the final month of her pregnancy, Dali stops transporting the stones and limits herself to looking after the cattle and milking the cows. One day, as she squats down, she feels the first pains of labour. Khamsu is out collecting wood at the edge of the jungle when he hears the cries of his wife. Terrified, he runs back to the village, but once in front of her, he panics. The contractions are getting closer and closer together, leading the future father to run around in all directions. He calls his mother and with a quiet authority, the old lady pushes him away, taking matters into her own hands.

Khamsu sits to one side and holds his rosary, imploring Buddha to make everything pass as it should. Dali's screams break his heart as his older brother and cousin come running over with a jar of *chang* to help get him through the ordeal. A long silence leads everyone to fear the worst, but suddenly, on this sunny October afternoon, the crying of a newborn baby is heard. Tears spring from Khamsu's eyes as he rushes over to his wife.

His mother, the baby's *hajur ama* (grandmother), hands over his son.

Overwhelmed, he declares, 'This child will have a great future. It's the will of the gods, I'm sure of it!'

Dali breastfeeds their still unnamed-son, and it will be seven whole days before the *lamas* baptize him Pasang Tendi. Pasang because he was born on a Friday, and Tendi because that is the name they liked. The *lamas* tell them that 27 October 1983 foretells a bright future. Who knows, perhaps Tendi might be the reincarnation of Rinpoche (an honorific term in the Tibetan language meaning 'precious', reserved for a reincarnated *lama*)? Deep down, Khamsu knows that his son will have an extraordinary future.

Over the next four years, Dali will give Tendi a sister and younger brother. Today, Lapka is married to Pasang Sherpa, a great summiter who works with Tendi. His brother Nima, meanwhile, is a monk and continues to follow his own long, spiritual path.

Tendi's earliest memories of his native village concern the final phases of his childhood home's construction. As a toddler, he accompanies his mother to the river every day, helping to transport the small stones used for the walls. His father makes him a miniature *doko* (a handwoven basket made from bamboo and held by a headband) in his size, and he is unfazed by the heavy loads, even taking it in turns to carry Nima and Lakpa on his back.

As Sherpas are generally poor craftsmen, Khamsu calls on a Rai mason to help once all the materials have been gathered together. A carpenter from a nearby valley also comes to fit the doors, windows and roof. In the middle of the room, a square patch of beaten earth serves as a hearth, and as both Khamsu and Dali are deeply religious, the house must also include a domestic altar. Khamsu always brings back various objects from his expeditions, such as dishes for offerings, incense, and photographs of famous *lamas*, including the revered Dalai Lama. His collection of prayers is placed respectfully on the altar, while Dali erects a *darchen* (a mast for hanging prayer flags) by the front door.

For the young family, this new home means a comfort they have never experienced before, and Khamsu, in particular, looks forward to the fact that they will be less cold in the winter months. Dali takes over cultivating the fields to bring more diversity to their vegetarian diet, and at 4 years old, Tendi helps with all the housework. With no official education or school, all children work full time for their parents and the rest of the family.

CHAPTER SIXTEEN

STICK OR TWIST?

IT IS 1990. LIKE MANY Sherpas, every year, towards the end of September, Khamsu leaves his family and heads for the capital, Kathmandu, to join one of the various trekking companies. A dedicated *sirdar*, he is easily able to find work and often goes on three expeditions in a row. The money he earns allows him to buy clothes and food that significantly improves his family's standard of living. He spends the winters in the village, but in March, he eagerly returns to Kathmandu. There are not as many trekking expeditions in the spring, meaning there are much more people looking for work. Once there, he often receives the cold shoulder: most of the positions are already taken by Sherpas domiciled in the capital, or by those who have arrived before him. All this means that Khamsu has to be content with menial jobs that are more painful and certainly not as lucrative. For some time now, however, an idea has been forming in his mind: why not settle in Kathmandu in order to be hired more easily on major expeditions?

Life in the valley is particularly trying during the monsoon; the rains are heavy and leeches are everywhere. The villagers live in constant fear that wild animals will ransack the gardens, and although the lands surrounding Saisima can produce corn, barley, potatoes, and other vegetables, it is not enough for what the people need, not to mention the fact that there is very little variety in what they eat. Consequently, rice and lentils have to be purchased from the Rai farmers further down the valley, but many of the families there are often living on the edge themselves, so have nothing to sell anyway.

This means the people of Saisima must travel further afield, to the rich rice fields of Imchung or even the district capital of Khandbari. Heavily laden, whole families often set out on these journeys, covering great distances walking from dawn to dusk over two or three days. When the harvest has been generous, they use potatoes as currency. As a child, Tendi has a certain pride in participating in these expeditions, always making sure the load he carries is compatible to his age.

How can one not dream of a better life when faced with such harsh conditions? Khamsu is obsessed with the idea of settling in Kathmandu, although he has still failed to mention the subject to Dali, his wife. Constantly weighing up the pros and cons, he returns to Saisima after a season of trekking to find Dali seriously ill and bedridden. The *lamas* arrive to say their prayers and a *dhami* (shaman) even decides to sacrifice a hen. Dali recovers slowly, but Khamsu is convinced his wife's illness is linked to an error he allegedly committed during his last outing. Consumed with terrible remorse, he begins to pray even more than usual and spends a lot of time at the *gompa* in the hope of being forgiven, as well as praying at the family altar at home.

Tendi has just turned 7 and helps to look after the herds out in the pastures at the edge of the jungle. He likes working in such close proximity with nature, learning to identify edible berries he can eat in the fields and bringing home mushrooms for his family. It is clear to Khamsu, however, that without an education, Tendi will have to be content with following the same path as he has. Knowing how difficult it is to climb the career ladder when you struggle to read and write, this vision of his son's future haunts him. One day, he decides to speak to Dali about it:

'Tendi has to go to school. It's clear he's smart.'

Unfortunately, the nearest school is two days' walk from the village. Tendi is thus entrusted to a Sherpa family who live less than an hour's walk from the school. To pay for his board, they agree he will help out with the household chores: doing the dishes, assisting with the cleaning and fetching wood for the fire, and will not be allowed to go to school until such tasks are completed. For two years, Tendi tries to make the most of his part-time schooling, but still manages to progress. Alas, working with students from other Rai and Tamang ethnic groups does not go well. He is often pulled to one side and called *Bothe*, a name given to immigrant Tibetans in Nepal. Despite regularly being hit by older children, he never dares to complain and once every three months is able to return to Saisima.

Seeing how unhappy he is, his parents enroll him in the local monks' school, where he spends five years learning the sacred texts alongside older children. The monastery is run by his great-uncle and grandfather, who are both *lamas*. Dressed in their burgundy robes, the children practice reading and writing mantras every day from 9 am until 2 pm. From the start, Tendi is passionate about studying Sanskrit, taking care to inscribe 'Om Mani Padme Hum' on the stones in order to reinforce its protective effect. By reciting the mantra over and over, he invokes the powerful and benevolent attention of Chenrezig, who embodies the compassion of Buddha.

Once the fundamentals have been learned, the children sing the hymns in the same voice, sometimes for hours on end. The rhythm plunges the young students into a trance-like state, where no outside thoughts can penetrate. When they finally emerge back into full consciousness, they feel imbued with peace and serenity. Later, Tendi will be joined on the *gompa*'s benches by his younger brother, Nima, who will devote his life to prayer.

The family home breathes with the rhythm of the Buddhist rites, with everyone feeling spiritually fulfilled. Khamsu, meanwhile, is still persisting with the idea of settling in Kathmandu, even though he knows most of the Sherpas who live in the metropolis do so in complete misery. The income he receives from three or four months of expeditions is not enough to pay for housing and support an entire family. A few Sherpas have even set up their own business, but competition is fierce and success uncertain.

Kathmandu is full of hospitals and doctors, but how can one access the care available without money? Khamsu is particularly conscious of Dali's fragile health, knowing if they stay in the village, they will have no choice but to call a healer if she falls ill again. Such people often take advantage of the innocence of the locals, managing to exploit them for all they are worth. Their usual method is to order an animal sacrifice, which is condemned by the Buddhist religion. As if that were not enough, they also have no qualms about taking the meat given as an offering for themselves.

The arguments in favour of a move to Kathmandu are becoming stronger. If they stay in the village, it is impossible for Khamsu to prove his skills and forge bonds of trust with the expedition bosses – a *sine qua non* (essential) condition if you want to be hired as a *sirdar*. His mind is made up, but Dali begs him to wait a little longer.

CHAPTER SEVENTEEN

TENDI: SHERPA

TENDI IS 13 WHEN HE first visits the capital, his big brown eyes glued to the bus window so as not to miss anything of this human anthill. Never in his life has he seen so many people and vehicles. His brain desperately tries to register everything as he asks 1,001 questions to his father.

Leaving the bus, the initial contact with the bitumen pavement surprises him. Tendi has never worn shoes before, but Khamsu pulls him by the arm telling him that walking barefoot is no longer an option. He has saved a dollar, a large sum of money at the time, intending to buy Tendi his first pair of shoes, judging that he will need them if he wants to start work as a porter. Before he knows what is happening, the young teenager is leaving a small shop in the Thamel district, smiling and wearing sandals. Immediately, however, his face tenses up; with each step, the straps get in his way, his heels feel like they are on fire, and his toes slip out. He ends up walking like a duck and after an hour of wandering the streets, large blisters have started to form.

His father has arranged for him to work as a porter with an organized expedition in Langtang, a region near Kathmandu. On the first day, Tendi puts his new sandals at the bottom of his *doko* and continues barefoot. Although not very tall, he is already very strong and the *sirdar* entrusts him with a load of around 20 kilos. During the twenty-six days of trekking,

Tendi tries to learn as many English words as he can, and one of the clients even teaches him how to write his name in Latin script. Before now, he has never written anything other than sacred texts in Sanskrit. As soon as he can put down his pack, he practices writing the letters T E N D I with a sharp pebble on nearby flat stones, and soon he is able to pronounce a few simple sentences.

The changing terrain forces him to concentrate more on where he places his feet. He puts his sandals back on when they cross a pass at 5,400 metres, but the feeling is even worse than walking barefoot. The soles have no grip, and he constantly twists his ankles, meaning the rest of the expedition turns into a bit of a nightmare. He receives around $30 for his work, but since he has to use this to pay for food, there is not much left over afterwards. Nevertheless, he is determined the remaining money will pay for English lessons as soon as he returns home.

A year later, Tendi is hired as a porter for an expedition lasting several weeks in the Khumbu region, in the very heart of the Sherpa lands. Arriving in the valley, he marvels at the towering peaks, with Everest standing before him, majestic. He thinks back to what his grandfather taught him: for years the Sherpas never climbed the mountains because they were the domain of the spirits and the gods. Now, at 14 years old, he knows that one day he will be working up there.

His young age and friendliness are major assets for forging ties with foreign tourists. The following season, the head of an agency offers him a job that seems perfect for him. Four German tourists have organized an expedition without a guide and are looking for a porter to carry their luggage: 5 kilos per person, 20 kilos in total. He will be paid 400 rupees ($3.50) a day, plus, he hopes, a generous tip at the end.

The expedition will take place north of Kathmandu, in the Helambu region, and promises to be relatively easy, short and varied. The Germans plan to sleep in lodges, which avoids carrying any heavy camping equipment, while the path itself winds through forests of rhododendrons and green bamboo, with no great increases in altitude. Tendi always enjoys passing through the lands of the Tamang and Yolma tribes, meditating at the many temples and monasteries to be found along the way.

From the start, however, the reality is quite different. In the absence of a *sirdar*, the tourists divide the responsibilities up among themselves. Without asking, the Germans inform Tendi that he is to carry all the equipment, which turns out to be much heavier than the promised 20 kilos. Tendi dare not say anything and realizes they will be sleeping in tents rather than lodges. Sheepishly, he tries to load the huge bags onto his *doko*, but the walkers are already impatient to get going.

The load is so heavy that the 14-year-old cannot walk at a brisk pace and struggles to keep his balance. The path climbs in steps along a water pipe, each pace requiring a great deal of effort. Tendi is used to being a porter, but in this instance feels more like a beast of burden.

After passing through the last village, the path enters the jungle and improves slightly. Unfortunately, the clients are advancing too quickly and Tendi can no longer keep up. He hurts all over and every stride brings fresh torture. The muscles in his neck start to cramp. He leans forward, trying not to concentrate all the weight on his head. His lower back is on fire, and he desperately looks around for somewhere he can put down his pack for a moment. Finally, at the top of the climb, he manages to find a suitable place to stop. As he does, he realizes the tourists have long since left his line of sight and undoubtedly have a good head start on him.

Once he has crossed the ridge, Tendi heads towards a village where the walkers are sat, exasperated, waiting for him. One man voices his displeasure, not in English, but in German. Tendi does not know how to reply. Showing no further concern for their young porter, they set up their tents while Tendi finds refuge for the night in a nearby house. Disgusted by their behaviour, he struggles to fall asleep. He begins a cycle of deep breathing while visualizing the goodness of Buddha. Half an hour later, finally calm, he drifts off to sleep.

The next day, his body still bruised by the efforts of the day before, Tendi struggles once again to keep up with the tourists' furious pace, and it is not long before he loses sight of them once more. Not knowing the route, he is forced to ask local inhabitants he meets if they have seen four Westerners pass by. Arriving late at the end of the stage, he is once again exposed to their remonstrations. On the third day, in the jungle, far from any village, Tendi arrives at a fork in the path. Which way? The group have left no indication of which path they've taken so, at random, he chooses the one on the right.

After an hour's walk, he finally reaches a village and asks if anyone has seen the foreigners. The answer is no. He retraces his steps to the trail crossing and this time takes the left-hand path. But night is falling and without a headlamp, he cannot see where to put his feet. Suddenly, he stumbles and finds himself sprawled on the ground, crushed by his load. Exhausted, tears flow down his cheeks. He tries to pick the pack back up, but is paralyzed by his sobs. He knows he needs to calm down. What would his uncle, the *lama*, do in such a situation? Taking a deep breath, he holds his chest upright and begins to recite the mantras, repeating his 'Om Mani Padme Hum' over and over in the coldness of the inhospitable forest. Concentrating on his breathing, he slowly finds the energy he needs,

A little calmer, he resumes his journey. How long did he stay there for? He cannot tell, but it was clearly too long for the walkers, who are waiting for him resolutely at the next camp, frozen with cold because all their warm clothes are in the packs carried by Tendi. When they finally see him appear, they are furious. Screaming and brandishing threats, one of them even grabs Tendi and shakes him, roughly.

Seeking shelter for the night, Tendi meets a friend of his father's, and, with a lump in his throat, tells him what has happened. The following day, the Sherpa approaches the Germans and tells them to hire a second porter immediately. From then on, carrying half the weight he had to before, everything becomes easier for Tendi. Even so, the rest of the expedition will remain unpleasant, as he continues to be scolded and threatened at every opportunity.

CHAPTER EIGHTEEN

EXODUS TO KATHMANDU

BEFORE LEAVING FOR KATHMANDU, KHAMSU entrusts the care of the cattle and land to those staying behind. It is a solemn moment when he finally closes the door of the house he built with his own hands. A few of the villagers gather around to wish the little family good luck, while the nuns bless the children and Khamsu checks the baggage one last time. He is convinced that leaving is the best solution, yet he knows leaving Saisima is breaking his wife's heart.

At 17, Tendi takes charge of the heavy and bulky luggage. Nima, two years his junior, also carries several items. Already very pious, he recites prayers along the way, which seems to lighten his burden considerably. Lakpa is 13 and has made herself her own *doko* for her personal belongings. Suitably loaded up, the Sherpa family walk for seven days before arriving in Hile, where they catch the bus. Lakpa climbs to the back and immediately snuggles up to her mother, having never seen so many people before. With an indescribable racket, the crowded vehicle sets off, rocking from side to side along the heavily rutted road. Sat on the roof, Khamsu and the boys cling to the iron bars to which the luggage is firmly attached, laughing as they bounce several centimetres up in the air every time they drive over a pothole. It will be almost twenty-four hours before they finally reach Kathmandu.

In the year 2000, the capital city is hardly somewhere you would want to live, with the 700,000 inhabitants making it feel like an anthill. The overpopulation stems from when the country was opened up in 1951 after the fall of the Rana dynasty, which had previously headed a totalitarian regime for over a century. Since then, Tibetans have arrived in large numbers, as well as Indians from Uttar Pradesh and Bihar, who have all found work on the various construction sites. After Sir Edmund Hillary and Tenzing Norgay conquered Everest in 1953, the tourist business has continued to increase. Kashmiris have also moved here to try their luck, not to mention Sherpas, who have also left their valleys behind. In fifty years, the metropolis has developed in a way that is as rapid as it is anarchic.

The savings Khamsu earned during his last season on Everest allow them to rent a maisonette in a working-class area of the capital. Dali is less than impressed. The building is dilapidated. The walls cold and damp. There is no electricity or running water. If you want to go to the toilet, you have to walk down to a small river, strewn with rubbish and excrement. They sleep on the floor that first night, huddled together to keep warm. Tendi comforts his little sister, who is crying as quietly as she can so as not to upset her mother any further.

As expected, their new life is difficult. Very quickly, the meagre rations they have melt away like snow in the sun. Food is scarce. The idea of growing and harvesting your own vegetables in a garden, right in the middle of town, is a pipe dream. Everything must be purchased. Meals are systematically made up of potatoes or *tsampa*, with only spices adding a bit of colour to such bland dishes. Although she does not want him to go, Dali cannot wait for the new trekking season so that Khamsu can finally bring back some money.

Meanwhile, Tendi loves school and studies a great deal. In the evening, in the dim light of the oil lamp, he goes over his lessons and looks forward to improving his English. His father, who never went to school, only learned the sacred texts in Sanskrit and even after several years of practice, he still fails to understand Westerners and their language. Even so, he has great hopes for his eldest child.

Nima, the second son, is sent to a monastery in Kathmandu when he turns 15, on his way to his future destiny as a monk. It is a blessing for this deeply religious family, whose Sherpa tradition dictates that at least one child should devote their life to prayer.

Months pass and life is still hard. At certain times of the year, Dali notices that Lakpa has difficulty breathing and coughs a great deal. She first thinks it is bronchitis that she cannot seem to shake off, but her friends in the neighbourhood tell her that pollution is to blame. With the Himalayan range to the north and the Mahabharat to the south, Kathmandu is in the middle of a natural fortress that prevents polluted air from escaping, ensuring a thick fog often covers the entire city. The fumes burn off during the day, but weak winds bring the pollution back over the capital at night, and between the cars, trucks, tens of thousands of mopeds and smoke from factories, including illegal brick kilns, you would be hard pushed to find worse air quality anywhere else.

In summer 2001, Khamsu travels to Europe for the first time. He is meeting Saouji, his Swiss friend, who has asked him to be the official assistant caretaker at the Audannes hut, a 2,500-metre mountain refuge located above the resort of Anzère, in the Valais Alps. Although hard-working and grateful for the change of scenery, Khamsu struggles to communicate with the hut's visitors, not to mention trying to learn even the slightest word of French. Nevertheless, he continues to return every summer for several years.

With the money he brings back to Nepal, as well as the income generated by his various expeditions, Khamsu finally manages to cover the rent for a small apartment. The move delights everyone. Several other families live in the same building, and Dali is able to cook on the landing using a gas stove, with the communal toilets positioned on the ground floor. The following year, they move into a slightly more spacious apartment, with the ultimate luxury of a toilet on the landing! As his earnings increase, Khamsu continues to improve his family's standard of living, meaning Dali thinks less and less about returning to Saisima.

Over time, their financial situation becomes more and more comfortable, until they eventually have enough money to buy land on which to build a house. The monastery of Kopan sits on top of the hill that dominates their new neighbourhood in the eastern suburbs of Kathmandu, and Khamsu and Dali try to go there at every opportunity. Following their example, other Khembalung families have migrated to Kathmandu. This includes Tsiring, Khamsu's brother, who decides to abandon the village of Saisima after realizing there are no prospects for him there.

The lives of Khamsu, his wife and their three children have changed a great deal in just a few years. Their new house has three floors and a large terrace, where Dali and Khamsu spend a lot of time praying in their own *gompa*. They rent some of the ground floor to a Sherpa family, while the rest is used to store the agency's equipment. Tendi's grandmother and one of her aunts also live there at one point. The third floor of the house has a bedroom furnished in the western style and is reserved for visitors. Daily life is punctuated by various rites and every morning, the couple go around the rooms to light the incense.

The house is the symbol of Khamsu's success and provides him with the opportunity to show his deep generosity. Numerous visitors are invited both to eat and sleep, with various inhabitants from Khembalung regularly knocking on the door. It is not uncommon for Dali, assisted by Lakpa, to cook for more than ten people. Another time, a young Gurung man who needs hospital treatment stays with them for more than two months. The offer does not go down well with other members of the Sherpa community in Kathmandu, who frown upon inviting people from another ethnic group into one's home, even worse if they are of another religion. The house is spacious, however, and the Nepalese traditionally care little about personal comforts, happy to lie down anywhere, be it on a simple carpet or mat.

CHAPTER NINETEEN

IN SEARCH OF
A BETTER LIFE

IN AUTUMN 1998, TWO YEARS before his family move to Kathmandu, Tendi is working as a porter during an expedition to Mera Peak (6,476m). At 15, his voice has broken, his muscles have developed, and he has grown a few precious centimetres taller. It is on this expedition that he will meet the man who would become his mentor, and a second father to him. Armand grew up in a small village in the Swiss Alps surrounded by 4,000-metre-high mountains, almost all of which he has climbed. At 58, this is his first trip to Nepal, and he immediately falls in love with it.

Gyeljen, Tendi's uncle, is acting as the *sirdar*. One of the "modern-day" Sherpas, he likes to dress in new jeans, a US Navy sweatshirt and a pair of fake Ray Ban sunglasses. While his knowledge of the high mountains, snow and glaciers is not as good as some of the other *sirdars*, his resourcefulness and common sense are second-to-none.

It is during this expedition that Armand is given the name "Saouji", and if the literal translation of this nickname means "boss", it is mainly because Armand is often very managerial in his mannerisms. Nevertheless, his words are always said with kindness and ever since this moment, no one in the land of the Sherpas ever calls him by any other name. Unable to express himself in English, Saouji, meanwhile, decides to learn Nepali from this very first visit.

The stage to access the mountain takes them along rural, country paths. Every step is a blessing, and the tranquility, gentleness and beauty of the landscapes bring Saouji and his partner Nicole, "Saouni" (the female version of Saouji), unspeakable joy. The panorama is breathtaking, although it is not long before it starts to become steeper. One misstep could be fatal and extra care is certainly required as they proceed in their flipflops like tight-rope walkers.

At the end of the morning, as the group passes other tourists, one of the porters stops alongside the pair from Switzerland and puts down his pack for a moment. He looks them in the eye to get their attention, puts his hands together and bows slowly in a sign of respect.

Namaste!' he says, a wide smile lighting up his beautiful, young face. Saouji cannot believe that someone that looks as young as he does can carry such a heavy load, but the boy's relaxed features reassure him. Saouji hands him a flask of tea, which he politely declines, preferring instead to drink water from streams. He does, however, accept some dried fruits before extending his open right hand, and resting it on the left. For Sherpas, such a gesture of greeting, offering or acceptance is never inconsequential, and as the young porter beams back at him, Saouji is struck by the charisma, almost mystical magnetism, he exudes. In camp that evening, Gyeljen tells him that the young man is Tendi, his nephew. It will be two years before they cross paths again.

In the meantime, Gyeljen offers Saouji and Saouni an unprecedented trek, far from the major tourist circuits: a journey to the wild Khembalung Valley, where the whole of Tendi's family is from. It will take them five days of walking to reach the hamlet of Saisima, which the Swiss couple have already heard so much about.

A few stone houses can be seen on the hillslopes of this remote and charming valley. The surrounding vegetation is dense, but the view unobstructed. It has been two years since Gyeljen has returned to his native land, and the first person to welcome the party is one of his sisters-in-law, Sikima. They greet each other with their hands clasped in front of their chests, bowing their heads, with no physical contact. She offers them *chang*, which Gyeljen immediately accepts. The couple, meanwhile, politely decline, preferring their tea.

The house is dark and cold. In the middle of the room, a fire crackles. Sitting on the floor, the children observe the strangers through the thick smoke. Suddenly, a short, old woman bursts through the door. It is Gyeljen's mother. She stares at them for a while, then gives her son's head a tender clout, taking his hands in hers. Their foreheads come together and press against each other in an embrace that goes on and on. Soon, everyone in Saisima has been reunited, although in truth this hardly amounts to more than five or six people. Gyeljen begins handing out the clothes the Swiss couple have brought, including socks, underpants, sweaters, and warm jackets.

The next day is *Gai Tihar*, the cow festival, where everyone goes to the *gompa* to attend a religious service. Villagers put flower necklaces around the necks of the cattle and give them salt. After all, the cows are the toast of the party! Nostalgically, Saouji thinks back to his childhood, when the cows were taken out to their summer pastures. Unlike his home back in Switzerland, the mountain pastures here have not been transformed into ski slopes, and it makes him feel even more attached to this remote corner of the world.

Back in Kathmandu, Gyeljen finds his nephew on a terrace in Durbar Square and tells him about his latest project. With the help of Catherine, his new English girlfriend, he wants to set up a local trekking agency, which he says will help secure the family's future. He will run the company, while Khamsu will plan the expeditions. Tendi drinks in his uncle's words, and it is not long before an astonishing flyer appears showing the two brothers, Gyeljen and Khamsu, in suits and ties, arms raised, on top of a mountain. Unfortunately, the agency is unsuccessful and Gyeljen leaves his wife and their four children to follow his British beauty to London.

In 2002, the political situation is tense throughout Nepal. The civil war between the government and the Maoist rebels is raging, meaning in some areas, tourist numbers have dropped by half. All the same, the situation fails to deter Saouji and Saouni from supporting their friends and on this latest trek, Khamsu wants to allow Tendi to discover the tricks of the trade. In fact, it is not long before the father starts to step back, leaving his son to manage most of the programme.

On one particular day, after four hours on the road and passing through around ten police checks, the group arrive in Trishuli Bazar. Horrified, Tendi discovers that the village has been burned down. The Maobadi (members of the Nepalese Maoist movement which provoked a civil war from 1996-2006 killing more than 10,000 people and causing a strong migration from rural areas to the capital), having apparently destroyed it in retaliation for the help the villagers allegedly provided to the army. In such a situation, the logistical side of the expedition is a heavy responsibility for Tendi. Yet despite his eighteen years, he is still able to impose his authority both on the group and against the armed militiamen, even though he has to pay them substantial bribes so as to be allowed right of way.

In spite of the ongoing political and economic insecurities, Saouji encourages Khamsu to set up his own business. No need to worry about attracting clients; he will take care of that. So, in 2005, Audantrek is formed, so-called in reference to the mountain refuge where they cemented their friendship four years earlier.

Over time, the business is gradually handed over to Tendi, and thanks to Saouji's sound advice, the young Sherpa develops a spirit and ethos based on respect and sharing. He retains a team of Tamang porters, who are able to stay in their village until the start of the season and are thus less tempted to settle in town. During the monsoon, the Sherpas living in Kathmandu are often idle, and it is practically impossible for them to find a permanent job. Tendi uses the time to concentrate fiercely on his English lessons, while also managing to get a small job in a coffee shop.

The relationship between Tendi and Saouji becomes closer with each visit. Consequently, Armand decides to offer him the position of assistant caretaker at the Audannes hut, even though Khamsu is still keen on his stays in Switzerland and is unwilling to give up his place. He sulks a little when Saouji asks him to sacrifice his position for Tendi, but soon recognizes that such a move will undoubtedly open doors for his son.

CHAPTER TWENTY

THE AUDANNES HUT

FOLLOWING HIS UNCLE AND FATHER, Saouji believes that Tendi's time has finally come. So, in the summer of 2004, Armand invites him to Switzerland.

The Audannes hut is located at the foot of the Wildhorn, a glacial peak 3,248 metres above sea level, able to accommodate around thirty people. The white, corrugated iron building overlooks a small mountain lake, approximately two and a half hours' walk from the ski resort of Anzère.

At 22, Tendi immediately proves to be very efficient at his job. Running an altitude refuge such as this is no easy task, and each employee has their own essential role to play. The working day lasts from 6 am until 10 pm, with breakfast needing to be ready before the customers leave for the Wildhorn. After this, tables must be cleared, the dishes washed, the beds made, not to mention the thankless task of cleaning the toilets every day. Tendi insists on doing the latter most of the time, but Armand prefers to take care of it himself, not liking to impose such a chore on others. Preparing meals takes several hours, and Tendi quickly becomes an expert in potato peeling. As a vegetarian, he struggles to understand why Saouji cooks so much meat, being quite content with soup and rice for himself.

Tendi is eager to learn French and so when the hut is not as busy, he fills notebooks with vocabulary and grammar exercises. He practices speaking with Saouji, inventing various scenarios that require specific words or phrases. Having already climbed Everest three times, he makes it a point of honour to recount his exploits in French whenever one of the clients asks about it. And even if the story takes a while to tell, his audience drinks in his words, willingly. He is even becoming a bit of a tourist attraction himself, with more and more people travelling up to Audannes to meet him.

One July afternoon, Armand heads down to the town to run errands. This usually takes all day, with the supplies later being transported back by helicopter. In Armand's absence, Tendi is alone at the hut, and although the sun is hiding behind the clouds, the temperature remains mild. The last guests have left and no one is booked in for the next night. Tendi has not had time to climb the Wildhorn yet, but with only 740 metres separating the hut from the summit, he thinks three hours should be more than enough time for him to make the round trip.

He travels light, perhaps even intending to set a speed record. The first part of the route winds up a steep, dirt road, but with a good pair of calves, the task is completed in barely thirty minutes. The view from the Col des Eaux Froides is usually spectacular, but today it is obscured by the fog, making it difficult to see the mountains nearby. The intermediate part of the ascent requires more concentration. Red markers painted on the *lapiaz* (moon-like stone slabs) are spaced at specific locations along the way. Unfortunately, Tendi misses some and is forced to retrace his steps until he finds one again, and it is an hour before he reaches the glacier. He immediately regrets not bringing crampons, previously believing them unnecessary as the glacier is not particularly steep and has almost no crevices. As he progresses, he slips on the ice, sometimes even falling down, with the rain that has begun to fall making the ground even more treacherous. His shoes have not been waterproofed for a long time and his feet are soaked. The temperature drops drastically as he realizes his jacket is far too thin to keep him from shivering. It is time to turn back.

With the fog thickening by the minute, Tendi can see nothing ahead but a huge expanse of grey in every direction. Lost on a mountain 3,000 metres above sea level, he is convinced his final moment has arrived. He finally reaches the hut after nightfall, where Armand, who has just arrived back himself, was preparing to launch a search party. Like a little boy caught with his hand in the cookie jar, Tendi admits that he had completely underestimated the climb. As far as he was concerned, the Wildhorn was just a small hill, not even as high up as the village of Namche Bazar! Saouji gives him a talking to, but above all promises to pass on all his knowledge of mountaineering. From now on, Tendi is committed to respecting all mountains, no matter how small.

Armand has never completed any formal guide training but has spent most of his life roaming the Alps. As an instructor for alpine patrollers and head of security on the ski slopes, rescues and avalanches hold no secrets for him. Together, they simulate accident situations, organize fake rescue operations, or diagnose and provide first aid to imaginary casualties. Tendi asks a lot of questions; his thirst for knowledge insatiable. Saouji is convinced that Tendi will make an excellent guide, but before that, he needs to know how to use a map and a compass.

In Nepal, none of his friends use Western methods to navigate their way around the mountains, instead operating primarily by relying on their instincts and experience. Saouji takes advantage of weather conditions similar to Tendi's disastrous Wildhorn adventure as practice. Map in one hand, compass in the other, he asks Tendi to find shelter through a fog thick enough to cut with a knife. Next, he asks him to guide him on the Tour du Wildhorn, a three-day hike linking several huts.

The apprentice takes his role very seriously and after three days of hiking in unknown terrain, has risen to the challenge perfectly. As soon as he can, Tendi goes on an excursion with the region's guides, who in return make him climb over rocks and allow him to use all the latest equipment. He takes charge of several expeditions over 4,000 metres, including the Dent Blanche (4,358m), a gneiss pyramid as beautiful and technical as the Matterhorn.

Tendi's address book gets thicker and thicker, and whenever he goes down to Anzère, everyone wants to invite him over. He discovers raclettes and fondue, but politely refuses dried meat dishes, one of the Valais region's great specialties. The locals always pour him a glass of wine, although his new friends always seem a little disappointed when he refrains from drinking with them. He often struggles to understand what is being said because they speak too quickly and with a strong accent. Instead, he simply smiles and says, 'Yes Didi', or 'Yes Daï' (Yes, Big Sister/ Big Brother).

In between his trips to Switzerland, Tendi attends the *Alliance française de Katmandou* (a French language school and cultural centre in the capital city), and regular customers back in Audannes are certainly impressed with his progress. Meanwhile, Saouji continues to teach him new mountaineering techniques as the pair review all the different kinds of climbing knots and types of tie ins. Sitting at the table in the canteen, Saouji scribbles down diagrams showing him how to use the haul system (allowing a load to be lifted using several strands of cable in order to multiply the tractive effort) and the self-rescues necessary for crevasse rescue. Standing in the middle of the room, Saouji next shows him how to cross a bergschrund (a crevasse that forms where moving glacier ice separates from the stagnant ice or firn above) using a tight rope and a short rope, then the ideal way to set anchors, belays and, finally, how to abseil properly. Outside, Saouji has fun hiding various barryvoxes (an avalanche victim detector) under the rocks, instructing his apprentice to find the devices in the shortest possible time.

Armand also introduces him to some big names in the mountain rescue community so that they can take him under their wing the following season. Now determined more than ever to become a high mountain guide, Saouji proudly encourages Tendi in his quest and will even help finance his training.

CHAPTER TWENTY-ONE

THE YETI

TO BE A GOOD GUIDE in Nepal, you must first become a *sirdar*. In 2007, a good reputation is enough to gain you the accolade, and Tendi has every intention of proving himself worthy. As his first official client, Saouji asks him to organize a several weeks-long expedition in the Khembalung, beyond Saisima, which they had already explored previously with Tendi's uncle, Gyeljen.

The adventure begins in Tumlingtar, a small town in the east of the country. Saouji arrives by plane, accompanied by a handful of friends from Valais. Khamsu is also there, and for this particular occasion, has agreed to let his son lead the way.

Tendi has already hired the necessary personnel for the expedition and arranged for the equipment and food to be transported by bus. Most of the porters come from Khembalung, and the climb along the endless valley proceeds smoothly, despite the bad weather. As the small delegation passes through the village of Yangden, Tendi proudly points to the school that has been rebuilt thanks to Nepalko Sathi, the humanitarian association founded by Tendi, Khamsu and Saouji. The structural work has been completed, but the rooms themselves still lack any furniture. The villagers gather in the square to thank the people behind the project, and in the general euphoria, Khamsu distributes various items of clothing collected in Switzerland.

The weather in the region is usually fairly settled in the autumn, but this year a persistent fog still clings stubbornly to the sides of the mountain. Leeches take advantage of the constant humidity to attach themselves to the hikers' legs. A recent landslide makes access to the nearby village difficult. There is a knot in everyone's stomachs as they cross the suspension bridge, which has been damaged by the torrent of water below. Wishing to thank the gods for allowing them to be able to cross over, Tendi turns the prayer wheel (a cylindrical metal wheel engraved with mantras) that sits at the entrance to Dobatak. The visitors pass proudly to the left of the *mani* wall (made of piled stones on which the mantra 'Om Mani Padme Hum' is painted), as required by Buddhist rites.

Dawa, a local porter from Dobatak, says that his father was a keeper at the Khembalung cave, the refuge of Guru Rinpoche, a reincarnation of Buddha. An important place for Sherpas, the cave is narrow and damp, but like speleologists (scientists who study caves), the men penetrate deep into the cavern to a source of sacred water. As Dawa begins to recite a long prayer, Tendi explains to the group that he has recently lost his mother after a serious illness. Sadly, the prayers recited by the *lama* from Saisima had no effect. Dawa had braved the storms to search for medicine in Gonthala, but the valley was impassable in the middle of the monsoon. After hours of battling the elements, he returned home with the precious medicine, only for his mother to die two days later in excruciating pain. '*Ke garné?*' Tendi says, 'Life is hard in this country!'

Another dilapidated bridge that threatens to collapse at any moment must also be crossed before reaching Saisima. The numerous *khata* (prayer scarves) hung on its railings are supposed to provide protection to users. Even so, Tendi almost lost his life at this exact spot. At just 10 years old, he had crossed the torrent to graze the cows on the other side and while playing in the forest, a violent storm had broken out. In a few seconds, huge downpours accompanied by lightning fell on the entire valley. The rumbles of thunder had overwhelmed him with fear, as the cows panicked and ran in all directions. When he tried to ford them across the river, one managed to escape and as the water rose faster and faster, the last animal was immediately swept away by the current as it tried to jump across.

Bravely, Tendi had climbed onto a rock and tried to jump over the tumultuous waves, thinking he would land on the other side of the shore, but his bare feet slipped on the soaked stones. Unable to swim, he was carried away by the torrent, trying desperately to cling to a rock or a branch, swallowing water and coughing as his strength failed him.

Believing his time had come, he miraculously drifted into a small cove where the currents were slightly calmer. Drawing on his last resources, he dragged himself on his knees towards a mound of branches, before finally fainting with exhaustion. His terrified father would later find him after a long search. Hoisting him onto the bank and realizing that he was still alive, he hugged his son tightly, crying bitterly as he did.

The monsoon brings risks every year, with many children dying or suffering an injury that can cause lifelong disabilities; the consequences of such as hazardous existence.

During the long days of walking, Tendi befriends Nicolas. This man from the Valais with a shaved head practices the same Buddhist rites as the Sherpas and Tibetans, and from then on, the pair meditate together at every opportunity.

After five days spent in the rain, their legs teeming with leeches, the team finally arrive in Saisima and set up camp near Khamsu's house. There is always a warm welcome in the villages, but the ceremonial drinking of the *chang* can pose certain problems, as Sherpas sometimes find it difficult to moderate themselves when the women bring out the drink in such large quantities. Unfortunately, it is not unusual for the Sherpanis to suffer the consequences from the results of their husbands drinking too much alcohol.

When they were at the Audannes hut, Armand often spoke to Tendi of this scourge, but the young man from Nepal had already known about it for a long time. After all, alcohol often flows freely in the mountains. A non-drinker himself, he authoritatively imposes a code of abstinence on his team until the end of the trek. Informed by the young *sirdar*, the local women instead return with milk and butter tea for the *"che che che"* ceremony, to the chagrin of certain porters, Khamsu most of all.

Despite the cold and bad weather, Saouji feels particularly happy in Saisima, as Tendi takes his second father by the arm and tells him, 'Saouji, this is where I was born. I was born in that house over there.'

Before leaving for their journey to the upper valley, the group heads to the *gompa* to attend a religious service ensuring the gods will look down on them during their expedition. The route begins with a particularly strenuous climb through the jungle, but the young *sirdar* takes care of everyone by maintaining a slow, regular pace. In the past, shepherds had used the path to lead their flocks to the high pastures, but the trail is now almost abandoned. At 3,800 metres above sea level, Tendi shows his group a rock shelter, known to the locals as the *lamani* (plural of *lama*) cave. He describes how, a long time ago, a nun was devoured by the Yeti, clarifying that the story is no legend, but a known fact!

Finally, the fog lifts to reveal the majestic Makalu, the fifth highest peak on the planet. Breathing soon starts to become more difficult for the Western members of the group, while the porters carry on ahead, whistling as they go despite their heavy loads. The Swiss have insisted on exploring more of these lands supposedly populated by monsters, ghosts and other demons. Marlène, a great connoisseur of nature and its benefits, practices shamanism and rejoices in the total immersion in this world of superstition and myth.

Generally, Sherpas avoid approaching lakes they believe to be haunted, and Tendi is hesitant to set up camp near their choppy shores. Unfortunately, it is hard to find better ground and as the sun sets, the surrounding 8,000-metre peaks are reflected in the water. By the fireside, in the light of the moon, he tells them a true story from the writings kept in the *gompa* at Saisima.

A long time ago, the lake next to them was inhabited by ghosts. Every evening at nightfall, the water swirled into giant whirlpools, and flames rose into the air before extinguishing. One September evening, a young shepherd boy who had ventured too far from home was lost forever, dragged into the depths of the lake. Fearing for the lives of their children, the villagers sought help from a *lama* who lived with his wife in a local cave. The holy man, it was said, had the power to cast out demons. The inhabitants of Khembalung welcomed the *lama* and his wife to Saisima, and the *puja* in the old *gompa* lasted all night. The cacophonous sounds of horns and drums spread throughout the countryside – possibly even frightening away the ghosts on the outskirts of the village as they did. It would seem the holy man certainly wanted to make sure luck was on his side. Boosted by the faith of the villagers and accompanied by his wife, the *lama* set off with a determined step towards the mountain. Barefoot, with no luggage or food, they walked briskly. Night fell as they reached the *lamini* cave. Sitting cross-legged, the couple tirelessly recited their mantras and at dawn, the man asked his wife to stay in the shelter until he returned.

Arriving on the ridge 100 metres above the cursed lake, the monk contemplated the body of water. It appeared calm, with only a few bubbles bursting on the surface. The ghosts were either resting or preparing for the hard battle that awaited them. The monk unfurled the prayer flags from one ridge to the other and set up a *chorten*. He also laid down a few offerings for the gods whose help he sought. In a trance-like state, he continued to recite the mantras until sunset.

As darkness quickly invaded the valley, he descended towards the lake, gesticulating and shouting commands as he went. He provoked the ghosts by insulting them and summoning them to leave their lair. Suddenly, a violent wind threw him to the ground, as the bubbles rising from the depths became more and more numerous. Steam shot up from the surface like a geyser and burst into flames. With the lake on fire, the monk once again rushed towards it. This time, an even more powerful dark force struck him down, forcing him to take shelter behind a rock. Under the wan light of the moon, the monk suddenly saw the emaciated limbs of the ghosts agitating the dark waters. Still uncertain of his victory, the monk resumed his litany. At the first light of day, he approached the body of water only to find that it had regained its tranquility. Three other lakes remained. The *lama* ran towards them, noticing with horror that the ghosts had also settled there. Armed with nothing but courage, he continued his ritual. After a merciless fight, the ghosts seemed to grow tired and resigned, promising that they would leave the little shepherds in peace. Two days later, back at the cave, the *lama* returned to find nothing but the shredded remains of his wife. She had clearly been devoured by the Yeti!

Tendi explains to his audience that the mountain is populated by good and bad spirits that must be respected, and that the rites they practice are there to appease their anger or implore their benevolence. The evening ends with Sherpa songs that create a raucous atmosphere and undoubtedly frighten away any spirits still present. In the early morning, the Westerners observe a few air bubbles bursting on the surface of the water. Nothing to worry about…

On the way back, the group passes another cave conducive to meditation. It is a place Tendi dreams of isolating himself in for several days when his schedule allows it. His great-aunt had recently stayed there for five weeks, even though it is also the place where the Yeti was last seen.

Shortly before Tendi was born, Phurba, his grandfather, who was also a *lama* of Saisima, had settled in the cave with four other monks for a long period of meditation before the arrival of winter. Snow had already covered the area and it was particularly cold. One morning, 100 metres from them, they saw a gigantic human form, its back turned, crouching down and facing the sun, its arms alongside its body and leaning on the ground. They could make out a pointed skull with long hair falling down over the shoulders, and large ears that moved in all directions, as if to pick up any sounds. Luckily, the creature did not see them, and the terrified monks took off towards the valley. His grandfather and his companions had seen the Yeti. Thanks to this story, there is certainly no doubt in Tendi's mind that the abominable snowman exists!

The young *sirdar* tells the group that in 1960, Sir Edmund Hillary organized a ten-month expedition to shed light on the legendary Yeti and visited several temples that were supposed to house relics of the creature. After scientific analysis, however, everything pointed to the conclusion that they were nothing more than the remains of bears and bovines. Despite the huge respect Sherpas have for the New Zealander, most still believe the Yeti is anything but a legend.

Back in Kathmandu, the Swiss provide a debrief on Tendi's first expedition as *sirdar*. They appreciated the pace set and the cultural dimensions of the trip, especially its "discovery" side. One woman even specifies that she had felt like the Buddhist Belgian-French explorer Alexandra David Neel as they progressed through the secluded lands. The only downside, they declared, was that comfort remained rudimentary and they would have appreciated a few amenities such as stools and a table. The food could also have been a bit more varied. Pleased with their report nonetheless, Tendi flashes a huge smile and promises to do better next time.

CHAPTER TWENTY-TWO

OBJECTIVE: MOUNTAIN GUIDE

THE RESULTS ARRIVE BY MAIL. Unable to stand the tension, Tendi asks his mother to open the envelope for him. With the letter in her hands, Dali immediately jumps for joy. At 24 years old, her son has just obtained the best result for the selection process at the ENSA (*Ecole Nationale de Ski et d'Alpinisme*), the prestigious French National School for Skiing and Mountaineering. Its instructors have recently set up a multi-year programme in Kathmandu for Nepalese who want to become mountain guides. Competition is fierce throughout the course, with candidates eliminated at each stage. In addition, there are those who are quick to remind Tendi that he only briefly attended school and can barely read and write.

But despite his academic and technical shortcomings, Tendi's motivation is limitless. He first needs to learn about wall climbing and be able to lead with a grade of 6b (an above average grade in terms of difficulty) on an equipped route. He trains every day on a cliff in Balaju Park, not far from Kathmandu, familiarizing himself with increasingly difficult routes and even buying a motorcycle to help him save precious time when travelling back and forth.

During his two years as an aspiring guide, his instructors observe his rock and ice climbing abilities, subjecting him to real rescue situations where he needs to demonstrate his skills. To complicate matters further, training takes place outside the trekking and expedition periods, either during the monsoon, or in the middle of winter when it was cold and damp.

In 2008, at the same time as he is accepted into the ENSA, Tendi renews his contract with the Benegas brothers and the company, 'Mountain Madness'. Tendi now has the opportunity to help prepare clients for what they are about to face, explaining to them the importance of stopping at each stage, just as you would do when scuba diving. He is also responsible for training the porters because they, too, need to comply with the company's safety rules.

Willie Benegas can clearly see how much Tendi has matured and finds the aspiring guide's way of communicating very appealing. The clients appreciate the explanations that accompany each demonstration, particularly those concerning their safety, learning that above 7,000 metres, the consequences of poor oxygen use can be dramatic.

This particular year, conditions on the Khumbu Icefall are predominantly stable, and Tendi realizes that he has been crossing it without even needing to pay much attention, meaning he is better able to assess future dangers, and in such good conditions, the 'Mountain Madness' team easily reach the summit of Everest.

On the way back, in the village of Pheriche (4,400m), Tendi is sleeping in a lodge with several other porters when someone shakes him awake sharply at 1 am.

'Tendi... Tendi... one of the porters is very ill. Come quickly! We don't know what to do.'

He hears one of the men laying nearby groan. Observing him in the light of his headlamp, he calls out to him, softly.

'*Bhai, bhai*, little brother'. With his ear to the man's chest, the gurgling noises he hears leave him in no doubt; the porter is developing a pulmonary edema. He knows there is only one thing to do: they must descend as quickly as possible to lose as much altitude as they can. He empties the contents of his bag and takes the man on his back – no small feat considering the man weighs at least 70 kilos. He constructs a canvas harness in the shape of a diaper (a D system learned during his training) to help carry him down, but even so, the jagged path from Pheriche to Pangboche is very hard work.

He has already been walking for four hours by the time the next day dawns. His patient periodically loses consciousness and slips to one side or the other, making his task even harder. Tendi still hopes that someone else will take over, but the porters who pass him are already very busy and unable to help. Meanwhile, none of the tourists seem to care about what is going on. Finally, after six hours of effort, Tendi arrives in Pangboche where he hopes to deliver the patient to the clinic, only to find it closed, with the stagnant layers of fog preventing any possible helicopter assistance in the meantime. Tendi asks two other Sherpas for help, but quickly realizes they are completely drunk and of no use anyway.

As the patient's condition deteriorates, the only way to save him now is to walk down to Tengboche. To do this, however, Tendi will need to walk further along the river and go over a suspension bridge. Upon their arrival, an expedition doctor is finally able to give the patient an injection. Despite his exhaustion, Tendi's greatest reward is to see the man smile at him and say thank you.

The following year, the future guide builds up his medical knowledge even more, moving from theory to practice in the middle of the death zone. Descending from the summit, he sees a man lying in the snow below the Hilary Step. Members from other expeditions continue to pass by with complete indifference, so Tendi quickens his pace to reach him. He kneels down and raises his thermos to his lips before regulating his oxygen flow and finally forcing him to get up. A small, descending group stops to help and they soon learn that, having been too slow in his ascent, the poor man had been left alone while his companions continued their advance to the summit. If it had not been for Tendi's intervention, he would be dead.

In 2015, Tendi passes his final exams with ease. Now he is a recognized mountain guide throughout the world. Even so, he has to wait for the creation of the association of Nepalese guides recognized by the IFMGA (International Federation of Mountain Guides Associations), to officially receive his certificate. Still under the control of Western guides in the meantime, the new Nepalese guides instead provide training for other aspiring leaders.

To celebrate his achievement and to thank Buddha for his protection and guidance, Tendi decides to make a solo, winter ascent of Ama Dablam in record time! Back in Switzerland, Armand receives the following text message from him: 'I'm at 6,812 metres on the top of Ama Dablam. *Namaste* Saouji!'

After his escapade, Tendi returns home, proud to have accomplished everything his father had dreamed of for him. Over the course of a generation, both working conditions and recognition of porters themselves have evolved unbelievably. To be sure, achieving the title of international guide would have been simply impossible for Khamsu, the small peasant from the Khembalung mountains.

PART THREE

PART THREE

CHAPTER TWENTY-THREE

TEMPTING FATE

IN THE SHERPA COMMUNITY, PARENTS perform the essential ritual of arranging their children's marriage at an early age. Khamsu and Dali want to find a wife for Tendi because, according to custom, a family is only complete once descendants are assured, and so a Sherpani must be found from another clan. In the past, children had no say in the matter, but now, the main stakeholders are consulted. Even so, it is not uncommon for them to accept a choice that is not always their own so as not to contradict their parents or from fear of suffering any reprisals.

Tendi meets the first girl Dali and Khamsu have chosen for him as a potential bride at an organized party in 1997, when he is 14 years old. The young girl's parents are traders and are comfortably well-off. It is hard to find a better match. Unfortunately, upon seeing his would-be bride for the first time, Tendi realizes that she is still only a child. Panicked, the teenager rebels against his parents and categorically refuses to engage in such a project!

From then on, every autumn, on his birthday, potential contestants parade through the house as different fathers seek to marry their daughters off at any price. Some offer substantial dowries, which is no small matter for Khamsu: 'Yesterday, I ran into Tsiring, from Solu. Remember him?

I met him on an expedition once. He's a really good guy and is eager to marry off his 16-year-old daughter.'

'I've told you a thousand times,' Tendi responds curtly, 'before even thinking about marriage, I want to become an international guide and the training will take several years.'

'But you don't need to do that! Our trekking agency is starting to do really well.'

'It's not enough for me. I've got other ambitions.'

'I warn you, if you wait too long there'll be no girls left to marry.'

'I don't care! I'm not marrying anyone until I'm at least 25.'

Tendi meets lots of single people over the age of 30 on his various expeditions, making him wonder why he, too, could not wait a little longer? Plus, he is disturbed to realize that some older clients like being with him, meaning he is often torn between (sometimes) reciprocal attractions and his attachment to Sherpa traditions.

Faced with the growing insistence of his parents, he calls Saouji in Switzerland to share his concerns, explaining that his desire to obtain his guide's license is much greater than his desire to chase girls. After hearing what he has to say, Saouji immediately telephones his friend Khamsu to persuade him to leave Tendi alone for a few more years.

Much to Khamsu and Dali's despair, their daughter Lakpa also resists this same pressure to marry. The truth is that she already has a secret boyfriend, but is afraid he will not be accepted by her parents. The man in question, Pasang, is a friend of Tendi's, and accompanies him on most of his climbs. Her brother is fully aware of the situation and even acts as an alibi so that the two lovebirds can see each other in secret.

But it is not just Tendi's parents who are trying to get him married off, his friends are getting in on the action, too! During a club night, Dorje tells him about his 18-year-old cousin whose marriage has recently been annulled. He hands Tendi her photograph, which he pretends to barely look at. However, the studio portrait of Phuru certainly makes an impression. Her almond-shaped eyes seem to light up her face, while her high cheekbones make her look like a model. Dorje informs him that her father is an Everest veteran, having summited the mountain twelve times, and that Phuru went to a good school and is now working in a travel agency. Tendi returns the photograph, telling him that he is not interested. Yet as the months pass, he often finds himself thinking of the face of this beautiful Sherpani and begins to get used to the idea that she could one day become his wife.

At 29, with his international guide certificate in his pocket and ten ascents of Everest under his belt, Tendi believes it is finally time to start settling down. His friend Dorje thus initiates a meeting that proves to be an incredible act of fate. It is *Losar*, the Tibetan New Year, and the main religious holiday of the Sherpas. As custom dictates, Tendi walks around the *stupa*, reciting mantras while spinning the prayer wheels. Ahead, he sees two young people walking slowly and decides to join them. One of them is Dorje, the other is the lovely young woman in the photograph. As the three of them move away from the flow of pilgrims, Tendi is left utterly speechless and filled with an intense emotion whenever he looks at this young woman, who lowers her eyes timidly. They greet each other, hands clasped on their chests: '*Tachidele … namaste*'. He invites them to sit down on a cafe terrace usually frequented by tourists. The drinks there are expensive (few Nepalese can afford them), but he is desperate to impress Phuru.

Despite her immense shyness, Phuru smiles broadly, before blushing and lowering her head again. Tendi can see she is embarrassed and so strikes up a conversation with Dorje to try to make her feel more at ease. He cannot believe how beautiful she is and would do anything to be able to reach out and take her hand, but he does not dare. Half an hour later, Dorje, who has engineered the whole thing, leads them to the nearby monastery where he has made an appointment with a monk. Before they enter, he turns to ask the two young people if they wish to proceed, and despite worrying that everything is moving too fast, Tendi is too afraid to say anything. He looks to see if Phuru will speak out, but she just nods shyly. Once inside, Tendi expects to meet an elderly monk, but to his great surprise, the man he sees is in his twenties. In fact, he is already acquainted with him because the monk happened to study with his brother, Nima. The monk welcomes them warmly and invites the couple to sit in front of him. In order to assess whether conditions are right for a good marriage, after murmuring a few mantras he proceeds to ask about their background and dates of birth. He then serves some butter tea and consults various documents. Then, after a long silence, he tells them, 'There's nothing standing in the way of your marriage, but you'll have to respect and be faithful to each other throughout your life. I give you my blessing.'

Leaving the monastery, Tendi delicately takes the hand of the young girl.

'Phuru, do you want to be my wife?'

'Yes,' she replies quietly.

'I've been waiting for this moment for a long time.'

During the weeks that follow, the lovers meet more and more often and get to know each other better. Tendi behaves like a true gentleman; his excellent salary allowing him to spoil his bride and meaning he can take care of all the little details. Phuru is head over heels. They discover they have lots in common, enjoy the same things, and have an almost identical outlook on life. Even though Phuru is more reserved by nature, Tendi manages to make her talk, listen to her, understand her and make her laugh.

Meanwhile, unbeknownst to Tendi, Khamsu, accompanied by five friends, visits Phuru's family. Questions fly from both sides. Khamsu wants to know everything about her family's background, what her parents do for a living, and the role that religion plays in their lives. For their part, Phuru's parents are worried about Tendi's job. Is it not very dangerous? Does he have a regular income? Will he be a good husband?

Luckily, by the end of the interview, everyone leaves smiling, convinced that the marriage will be a success.

CHAPTER TWENTY-FOUR

PHURU AND THE GIRLS

TENDI FINDS IT INCREDIBLE THAT even in 2012, he still has to ask for his bride's hand in front of a large audience. As is tradition, Phuru's parents have gathered friends and neighbours together, alongside other members of the family. More nervous than he has ever been before, Tendi makes his request in front of no less than forty people. Khamsu and Dali are there alongside him, sharing the moment they have been waiting for for many years. When the ceremony is finished, Khamsu confesses to his son that the two families had already consulted with each other. Now freed from any burden, the fathers of the engaged couple let the *chang* flow.

Shortly after their engagement, Tendi's work completely takes over as he embarks on multiple trips abroad. Months pass and Phuru begins to grow impatient that nothing will be done for their upcoming nuptials. She decides to visit a *lama* to determine a favourable date for the event, according to the Tibetan calendar, and two years later, on 26 November 2014, he finally blesses the couple. The intimate ceremony takes place in front of immediate family members only, with the monk sealing their union by placing a red dot on their foreheads. It is an extra emotional moment for the bride's parents, who will now see their daughter fly away towards her future.

Four days later, 2,200 people are invited to Tendi and Phuru's wedding – the two families were keen to bring together virtually the entire Sherpa community of Kathmandu! When they arrive, each guest receives a *khata* adorned with the eight lucky symbols. The newlyweds cause quite a stir. Tendi wears traditional dress consisting of a *tutung* (a long shirt crossed at the front), a *chuwa* (long coat) and a *shamo* (very similar to a cowboy hat). The bride, meanwhile, wears a magnificent yellow *bakhu* (the festive dress of the Sherpani), embellished with a *pandem* (a colourful woolen apron). On her head, a *washa* serves as a headdress and her elegant Tibetan jewellery sets off her special outfit even more.

The wedding is celebrated in the purest Sherpa tradition, that is until British pop music suddenly bursts from the speakers. Tendi handles himself pretty well on the dance floor, much to Phuru's delight. In the early morning, when the final guests have left, the young couple exchange sweet promises of a bright future together. Placing a kiss behind his wife's ear, Tendi reiterates his total commitment to their relationship.

The couple immediately move into the family home, where Khamsu and Dali let them occupy an entire floor, welcoming their new daughter-in-law with great respect and affection. Leo, a client that Tendi took to the summit of Everest, offers him two plane tickets to Buenos Aires. It is a dream gift for their honeymoon and the couple spend a month crisscrossing Argentina, which Tendi already knows fairly well having climbed Aconcagua several times. No ascent is planned for this occasion, however, with only cultural visits and the added bonus of a short stay in a ski resort on the agenda. A few years later, the couple have a romantic trip to New York, making unforgettable memories together as they discover the city hand in hand. On another visit to the United States, they are welcomed in Colorado by Tendi's great friend, Dave.

On 19 May 2015, the birth of his daughter Dolma makes Tendi a fulfilled man. Holding this tiny creature in his arms, he knows that Buddha will always be by her side to protect this newest member of their family. Fatherhood quickly transforms him, as his sense of responsibility, which is already very strong, is strengthened even more.

Phuru knows that her husband loves his profession, but that does not stop her being worried every time he leaves home on another trek. She continues to have sleepless nights, living in a permanent state of stress until he returns home. Tendi understands his wife's anxieties and tries to reassure her, but not always with success. He explains every detail of the expedition so that she can see how he is constantly trying to limit the risks involved, as well as lovingly joking about his clients and team members to make her laugh.

He shares everything with her, even though he knows that she suffers in his absences. This is why, whenever he is at home, he devotes all his free time to his wife and Dolma. He spends hours playing with his daughter and often takes Phuru out to a restaurant, treating her just like he did on that first day they met. Despite his busy schedule, he always manages to get away with them for a few days, ignoring many other invitations in the process. The feeling of being a devoted husband and father is further reinforced with the birth of his second daughter, Dechen, in August 2020. Returning from Antarctica, after having been absent for two long months, he offers his three loves a 'surprise safari' in the Terai, a lowland region south of the outer foothills of the Himalayas. It is another unforgettable trip and Dolma will always remember paddling in a canoe on the river and the wild animals they see up close.

Even though their life together is mostly harmonious, Phuru and Tendi still sometimes argue. One evening, Phuru asks her husband if he can take Dolma to school the next morning. Taken aback, Tendi looks at his wife wide-eyed. Surely she remembered that the day before he had told her his clients were arriving at 8 am and that he had to meet them at the airport? Phuru continues to argue her case, as the pair refuse to move from their respective positions. Tendi is used to providing his progamme in advance, believing preparation to be his best ally. Such a strategy often allows him to defuse many a delicate situation, but sometimes this is not always the case and it certainly does not appear to be doing so on this particular evening with Phuru. Without conceding, Tendi goes to find his mother, and, luckily, Dali will be able to take her granddaughter to school the next day.

Following this unfortunate episode, Tendi makes time to put things straight with his wife in order to diffuse the situation. Phuru is very upset. He sits down next to her, taking her hand and reminding her that she can always count on him 100 percent. He tells her that he is a serious and honest man, who never hangs out in bars or clubs, and who never drinks alcohol. He assures her, once again, that he would never look at any other woman. Phuru remains silent and continues to stare at the floor. Tendi goes on to remind her how vital the income generated by his job is, and how it allows them all to have the best possible future. He wipes away a tear that runs down her beautiful cheek, and the conversation ends with a long embrace. Tendi likes to say that Phuru is the fire and he is the water in their relationship; two opposing temperaments which, in the end, are the perfect foil for each other.

CHAPTER TWENTY-FIVE

YOGA AT 7,000 METRES

TENDI KNOWS THAT IF HE wants to amuse a crowd, all he has to do is mime the yoga positions performed by one of his clients on the slopes of Manaslu in 2014. The laughter is immediate, especially when he tries to do the splits. It is true that nothing could have prevented Olya Lapina from getting into positions such as the downward-facing dog, the warrior or the lizard. Yoga is a part of her every day life, no matter where she is or what other things she is doing. And so, at Camp 4 (7,400m), she embarks upon the slower-paced Yin Yoga, and with no oxygen, settles into asanas (yoga positions and meditation postures) for five long minutes before changing positions.

In October 2014, this 42-year-old American-Russian businesswoman is at the top of her game. Her preparation has been worthy of the greatest Himalayans, having trained for weeks on the Icelandic ice cliffs to test the various situations she might encounter in the Himalayas. Tendi is unused to having clients who are as well-prepared physically as they are mentally. For Olya, every detail counts. Three months before arriving in Nepal, she completely gave up caffeine, convinced that an unresolved addiction in extreme situations would disturb her mind. Food also plays an essential role in her balance and well-being. Like Tendi, she is a vegetarian and adapts perfectly to Nepalese cuisine. Then, thanks to yoga, she manages to master her breathing both in the high mountains and during deep-sea dives.

Their complementing characters work in their favour against the always unpredictable Manaslu. After meeting in Kathmandu, the bus drops off the group of foreigners in Besisahar, the starting point for the legendary Annapurna range. Led by Tendi, the team begins its long approach and acclimatization walk before arriving in Samagaun in full fog. The village seems to live in a perpetual period of slow motion during the monsoon months, and at 3,800 metres above sea level, foreigners, including Olya, find it difficult to warm up in the poorly insulated lodge. An hour later, the light rain finally stops.

Tendi leads the group past a *stupa*. He approaches the white altar, telling them that it houses old prayer books and adding that some *stupas* include the relics of great Nepalese monks. The visit continues at the monastery, where the central room is particularly colourful. Two wrinkled old women, their age impossible to guess, mumble mantras softly. Their eyes shine but their dirty clothes are worn out as they spin prayer wheels at high speed. It seems that this religious object allows them access to a certain wisdom – the most superstitious Buddhists always have one in hand.

The clouds finally part, giving way to a spectacular view of Manaslu. The expedition continues through a beautiful juniper forest, an emerald lake shimmering in the distance. The ascent to the last camp continues wonderfully, with each client taken care of by a porter. Shortly before midnight, Tendi and Olya prepare for their summit push. After wolfing down some Nepalese porridge and checking their equipment, the pair devote another ten minutes to meditation. In unison, mantras can be heard escaping from the small tent.

Reaching the summit is child's play for these two forces of nature, and at the end of the morning they are already back at Camp 4. Tendi still has to put away the equipment, so Olya takes the lead and goes to the lower camp alone. She does not feel that tired yet, even though she has already been walking for fifteen hours. She asks a friend from Quebec who made the summit the same day if they would like to accompany her, gently reminding her that it is never good to hang around at high altitude. The Canadian quickly agrees and the two women progress rapidly until they eventually find themselves trapped in the middle of impassable crevices, searching desperately for a way out for over an hour. After reaching Camp 3, Tendi is terrified to learn neither Olya nor the Canadian have arrived. He sets off to find them and when he finally sees them in the field of crevices, he calls out calmly, but seriously, 'Didi, I told you not to move from Camp 3. You shouldn't have left without me. It's so dangerous here!'

Far from the tourist trail, their adventure ends a few days later with a quick retreat to a monastery in the Manaslu Valley. Dressed in their burgundy robes, dozens of children welcome the two climbers by bowing with joined hands as a sign of respect. Tendi smiles at them, a hint of nostalgia entering his brain. The monks offer them tea with yak butter and lead them into the large prayer hall. Lulled by the mantras, Olya has been practising yogic meditation for a long time, but has never experienced such a deep connection to her inner being.

2014 will continue to be a year of successes for the American-Russian, who brilliantly rises to her challenge of achieving six climbs in six months: Manaslu (8,163m), Ama

Dablam (6,812m), Mont Blanc (4,808m), Elbrouz (5,642m) and Aconcagua (6,961m) twice. It was at the foot of the legendary Argentinian summit where Tendi and Olya had met a year earlier, in 2013. Tendi had just completed the climb with his clients when the young woman's group had to give up near the summit due to bad weather. Before returning to the United States after her successful ascent of Aconcagua in 2014, she arranges to meet Tendi in the city of Mendoza. Even though he had originally intended to return home after his latest, successful ascent, both he and Olya somewhat crazily decide to redo the Aconcagua, but this time taking the particularly difficult route via the Polish Glacier. The next day, they are back at base camp, where everyone they meet tries to discourage them, calling them suicidal and reckless.

On 8 March 1934, four Poles had reached the summit of Aconcagua by this steeper route, which had previously never been climbed before. Eighty years later, achieving this ascent is still no mean feat. Indeed, it is climbed less often than the popular Plaza de Mulas route, and a short time before, in January 2013, two Americans had tragically died there. Their bodies remain trapped in a crevice due to the fact that despite the insistence of their families, no rescuer wanted to engage in any salvage mission.

Animated by the same inner strength, Tendi and Olya are nevertheless determined to continue and feel fully capable of succeeding. Even so, they make a promise to turn back at a particular point along the route if their life is endangered, knowing that once they pass it, it is impossible to go back.

At 3 am, after a quick breakfast, Tendi and Olya get into their tent and sit cross-legged. Only a light wind can be heard in the total silence as they immerse themselves in deep meditation for ten minutes. Tendi sings Tibetan songs, joined by Olya, who proudly knows the lyrics. They know that it will take them at least sixteen hours of climbing to reach the summit – the record time recorded on this route. An ice axe in each hand, the two climbers progress along the ice cliff on the tip of their crampons for hours on end. There is no room for error. Tendi can tell that Olya is controlling her breathing better because they complete the ascent with no additional oxygen. As the cramps in their shoulders get stronger and stronger, the athletes manage to ignore the pain.

Next comes the dreaded passage through a narrow bottleneck wedged in a 50-degree ice face. The corridor is formed by the completely unstable masses of rocky islands on one side and clusters of seracs on the other, but the intrepid duo manages to cross it easily. Near the summit, a strong wind begins to gust. Even though Olya is exhausted, Tendi asks her to speed up as a threatening black cloud is heading towards the top of the mountain, and if it blocks out the sun's rays, the already extreme temperatures will drop even further. Their fingers are already in danger of freezing, which would make it difficult for them to use their ice axes. Worried, Tendi addresses his friend, saying, 'I'm going to pray for the clouds to change direction.'

Miraculously, a few seconds later, the cumulonimbus deviates from its trajectory. The worst is over. Mightily relieved, Tendi starts to hum Tibetan songs at 6,961 metres above sea level. After a few photos, he grabs his satellite phone and calls his father, who is desperately waiting for news back home. Proudly, Tendi tells him that he has just become the first person from Nepal to have succeeded in climbing this formidable route via the Polish Glacier. Olya Lapina, meanwhile, is the first American to achieve the same feat.

Taking the 'normal' route back, the descent is comparatively easy for our two heroes.

CHAPTER TWENTY-SIX

SKI RESCUER

IT HAS BEEN FIVE YEARS SINCE Tendi was last in Switzerland. Now, in the winter of 2016, Armand is waiting for him on the platform at Sion station.

'*Namaste*, Saouji!'

The two men hug each other tightly.

'It's great to see you here!'

Tendi is pleased to see that despite his recent hip surgery, at 76 this father-like figure is still very fit. His beard may have whitened, but there's not the slightest hint of baldness in sight.

On this occasion, Tendi will be in the country for five whole weeks, aiming to perfect his skills alongside the Swiss rescue elite. A young friend of his offered him his air miles so he could buy a plane ticket, while other friends are helping to finance his stay by covering the costs of his various training courses. The last week of his stay will involve an intensive course in mountain medicine, on skis. The only slight problem here, however, is that Tendi has never skied before in his life. Needing to learn in record time, an acquaintance gives him his first lessons on the beginner's runs at the resort of Anzère. His first attempts at snowplow turns are acrobatic to say the least, but when he falls down, he merely laughs out loud, declaring, 'I'm all white, just like the Yeti!'

A qualified instructor then takes over in the neighbouring region of Crans-Montana. His progress is fairly swift, even if his style still leaves something to be desired. The resort's rescuers allow him to accompany them on their missions, and one day, at the patrol station, the radio announces a woman has been injured on a blue run. While the rescuer grabs the stretcher, Tendi puts on his skis and follows him out, all the while concentrating hard on not falling down. When they arrive, it turns out the injured woman is English and speaks no French, so the ski rescuer asks Tendi to act as an interpreter.

'What's your name?'

'Charlotte.'

'What happened Charlotte? Are you hurt?' Tendi asks, holding her hand.

'I think I've torn my knee ligaments.'

'Don't worry, you're in good hands. My colleague is going to sled you down.'

Tendi helps to hoist her onto the stretcher, but unfortunately struggles to follow the convoy down the hill as his skis cross and he gets left behind. He admires the rescuer who skis quickly down to the ambulance already present at the bottom of the slope.

The next rescue involves a snowboarder who has managed to finish his race by careering into a tree. The man has injured his leg and is in a great deal of pain, so the rescuer immediately orders a helicopter equipped with a winch. Back in Nepal, Tendi is an expert in these 'long line' rescues. He looks carefully at the way the flight assistant carries out his task and notices that they seem to have a different way of doing it here. Five minutes later, the Air Glaciers helicopter lands on the Valais Hospital roof in Sion, where the snowboarder is immediately transferred to the operating room for a broken femur.

Tendi's observation internship continues in the emergency department; the nerve centre where all heli-ski accident victims come together. High season can be very busy and on weekends, when the weather is fine, dozens of stretchers clutter the hallways. The injured, many still with their ski boots on, wait patiently for their turn. A nurse is given the task of triaging the arrivals according to the seriousness of their situation. Falls, avalanches, hypothermia, altitude sickness, these are all scenarios Tendi regularly encounters in the Himalayas, where the rescue chain is often seriously clogged up.

He is fascinated by the coordination between the alert centre, where the initial distress calls from the area are received, the rescuers and the hospital. He notes that once the alarm has been sounded, the rescuers have six minutes to jump into the helicopter and reach the scene of the accident. Such a thing can often take several hours in Nepal, and the young guide dreams of one day importing such a system back to his home country. On his return, he decides, he will speak directly to the Nepalese Minister of the Interior about what can be done.

Meanwhile, still in Switzerland, he has now made enough progress on skis to risk the black runs, but an added difficulty awaits him during his last bit of training; the practical element of the exam requires him to go off-piste.

During the last week of the stay, his ski instructor drops him off in the small Valais resort of La Fouly. He takes the opportunity to speak with his guide, but François Mathey and his colleagues realize that it is going to be difficult to place Tendi in the right group. On the one hand, they are impressed by his Himalayan pedigree, but on the other, his inexperience on skis means he is not good enough to join the other guides, who will be carrying out rescue scenarios on slopes that are far too technical for him.

Instead, Tendi is placed with the doctors' group, who are also inexperienced in the mountains. The training begins with theory lessons, where he takes copious notes, concentrating hard. In the classroom, the other participants wonder what this Asian man is doing there, and so, rather shyly, Tendi steps up to introduce himself.

'Hello,' he says, 'it's nice to be here with you. I'm not a doctor, I'm a Sherpa!'

He goes on to explain how he wants to perfect his medical knowledge in mountain rescue, and rumours soon begin to circulate in the ranks that Tendi is, in fact, an Everest hero.

Alexia Willame, a young gynecologist, will be his partner for the week. Her aims for the course are the opposite of Tendi's. She's perfectly able to deliver a baby in the middle of the bush, but remains terrified of having to intervene during a race in the mountains, or even on the ski slopes, and so has signed up for the class in order to get out of her comfort zone. She tells him good-humouredly how when she skis with friends, she dreads arriving first at the scene of an accident, having no experience outside of a hospital of what to do with a dislocated shoulder or a broken leg.

Loving the mountains as she does, she believes it is important to know what to do if someone falls into a crevasse. Tendi makes it a point of honour to show her how to handle difficult terrain, and his advice is enough to give confidence to the young practitioner.

During the first lesson in the field, the trainees are asked to put seal skins on their skis, which provide better traction.

Despite never having used such things before, Tendi steams up a vertical slope, his speed amazing everyone in the group. Unfortunately, he soon becomes stuck as he realizes he does not know how to position his skis to change direction. However, it does not take him long to work out what to do, and he soon finds himself at the top of La Dotse (2,491m), where he stands, speechless, completely taken away by the beauty of the landscape. His companions are a little surprised by his reaction, especially given that their new friend is used to mountains over 8,000 metres.

If the climb was easy, Tendi will certainly remember the descent for years to come. François sets off first, leaving a magnificent track in the beautiful powder. Tendi tries to follow, but picks up too much speed and ends up spinning like a wheel and rolling into a ball of snow. Unhurt, he stands up and bursts out laughing. The guide then takes the time to explain different techniques to him so that he can control his skis a little better and therefore ski anywhere. Everyone in the group is impressed by the Sherpa's courage and how quick he is to pick up new things.

The practical side of the course consists of simulating real-life situations. Tendi already knows how to carry out crevasse rescues perfectly well, but his knowledge of snow science is somewhat limited, even though the slopes of Everest are often subject to avalanches. Doctors teach the group how to clear the airways and how to handle an unconscious person, while another instructor unwraps a Cervelas (a typical Swiss sausage about 12 cm long), cuts it, and pours a handful of dirt on what is supposed to be an open wound. One after another, the trainees are asked to find a solution to stop the bleeding, clean the wound and even stitch up the sausage. Tendi finds it hard to keep a straight face when it comes to his turn, finding the whole exercise rather amusing.

By the end of the course, the young man from Nepal has clearly united the team, and during the traditional party on the last evening, he ends up being the king of the dance floor, even launching into a demonstration of old Sherpa dances. The next day, everyone leaves with a heavy heart when it is time to depart. Alexia, who took the course to approach mountains and their dangers in a more thoughtful way, thanks her partner as she leaves, having made a new friend for life.

Tendi flies back to Nepal having made new friends and acquired the medical skills that might one day help make a difference out on his expeditions. His new training means he can return to the roof of the world knowing that now not only will his clients be safer, but he will as well.

CHAPTER TWENTY-SEVEN

NEPALKO SATHI

ON VALENTINE'S DAY 2022, SAOUJI hugs Nicole tightly before flying out to Kathmandu. Even at 81, the old man still has plenty of ideas in his head. Tendi picks him up at the airport where their reunion is, as always, tender and heartfelt.

Saouji does not like Kathmandu. It is too polluted, too noisy. Luckily, his stay there is only for as long as it takes to check the essential tools and equipment Tendi has purchased, which will then be transported to the Khembalung Valley.

Other friends from Switzerland in search of adventure regularly accompany the octogenarian to this lost corner of the world to do volunteer work. Renzo was supposed to fly out with him on this trip, but seventy-two hours before their departure, his Covid test came back positive, and it will be another two weeks before he finally arrives in Nepal on 3 March. Tendi, who never misses an opportunity to return to his childhood region, accompanies him on the journey. The bus drops them off at Katabahri, the last semblance of urban life, before disappearing into the endless valley.

Arriving in Sekhaya, the two men find Saouji in the company of Kibuti. In her thirties, she is dressed in traditional Sherpani costume and is holding a pitchfork in her hand. Saouji has just appointed her as the gardener responsible for the future 'Sky Gardens' in this town of 2,000 inhabitants. Tendi, who knows Kibuti well, welcomes the decision. A mother of two, she takes care of her children as well as looking after two others. With a husband who hardly works, her appointment gives her a new way of emancipating herself, and her motivation is limitless. In Nepal, women traditionally look after the crops, and selling them allows them to depend less on their husband's meagre income. In a few weeks, Kibuti has already proven herself fit for the role, while Renzo finally learns about the idea that Armand has told him so much about.

Back in 2017, Saouji had made the somewhat crazy bet of introducing the valley's population to the idea of permaculture (an approach to land management that adopts measures seen in flourishing ecosystems). Very fashionable in the West, it has the advantage of varying and densifying the harvests and when taking into account that at 2,000 metres above sea level, only barley, millet, potatoes and corn can be grown without too much effort, the local population is otherwise limited to growing these few food crops.

Saouji wants to encourage the Nepalese to eat more vegetables and plant fruit trees, which at present do not exist in the valley. In addition, these community gardens will also have the benefit of launching a new sector of activity in the region.

From the beginning, his aim is to involve the villagers in the endeavour to ensure their support for the project. He has brought along with him a broadfork, weeders, a hoe and a rake – all tools you cannot find in Nepal – and has chosen a piece of flat land in the village of Gonthala as the place for his first Sky Garden. Although he now no longer needs an interpreter, back in 2017 Tendi still acted as his translator, faithfully relaying to the inhabitants the spirit of this new kind of land management. Assembled together for the occasion, around fifty men and women listen to Saouji's speech before asking several questions. Unfortunately, some of them do not immediately grasp the reason behind changing practices that have served them perfectly well for generations. Others, meanwhile, who are perhaps a little more open-minded when it comes to modernity, promise at least to try. Whatever happens, it is certainly going to require a real effort to adapt to these new methods. Indeed, in these secluded valleys, no one has ever previously come to tell them how to cultivate their own vegetable gardens. The knowledge and know-how required has been transmitted down from generation to generation and, until now, has never been questioned. Faced with these new Western methods, the inhabitants must now wait to see what benefits can be derived from such a scheme.

In these isolated villages, the soil has never been contaminated by any chemical fertilizers or pesticides; an essential starting point for cultivating this initial 600m^2 area. According to the principles of permaculture, the vegetables need to be planted in mounds of natural soil, so Saouji alternates layers of foliage, finely cut wood, food waste and humus to generate a precious wealth of biotope. With the help of a hoe, several women draw a huge circle, out of which a multitude of branches spread out. Seen from the sky, the work takes the form of a giant mandala (a geometric configuration of symbols). Meanwhile, the men cut bamboo branches to make barriers 2.5 metres high. Arranged around the garden, these 'walls' will stop both domestic and wild animals from eating the crops. Nearby, a tool shed and chicken pen complete the new garden.

On inauguration day, the inhabitants of five surrounding villages come to sow the first seeds, including a group of nuns, whose modest lifestyle means they have very minimal needs. Others, meanwhile, who are more curious, celebrate the idea of discovering new things.

'This is the first thing you're going to eat: radishes,' Saouji proudly explains, a handful of seeds in his hand.

'And these are seeds for asparagus, squash, tomatoes, snow peas. Foodstuffs I'm sure are completely unknown to you.'

As Tendi finishes his translation, the eyes of all the villagers widen. The questions start to flow as Tendi acts as a transmission cable between this secluded world and that of his Western friends. At the end of a week of practical lessons on how to grow and maintain the crops, a paid gardener leaves to teach the same methods to those in several other villages, and once these modern techniques have been assimilated, most of the women will continue to practice them from then on.

Five years later, in 2022, several community gardens have been established in the Khembalung Valley. A Nepalese committee made up of a representative from each hamlet makes the link between the valley's inhabitants and Nepalko Sathi, although not everyone in the villages is fully onboard with the project.

In this spring of 2022, Tendi, Renzo and Saouji set off for Saisima, where they want to build a community farm in order to encourage young families to settle there. On their way, they cross one of the bridges their association has helped to finance, not to mention the path that has also been redone thanks to Swiss donors. Arriving at the hamlet, which is home to just ten inhabitants, including five nuns, they find the clearing work has already begun.

Saouji has been begging his Sherpa friends for years to keep cultivating their land and resist the lure of an easier life in Kathmandu, as most regions outside the tourist circuits continue to empty, inexorably. The Nepalese capital is full of Sherpas, Tamangs, and Rais, who all leave their valley due to the lack of any prospects. And while Tendi's career certainly reinforces the idea that success is possible if you settle in the capital, for every success story like his, thousands of others end badly. Living in the city with a dependent family is difficult, especially when the trekking season only generates a few months of income each year. All it takes is a serious incident or an event like the Covid-19 pandemic to plunge these exiles into a genuinely precarious state.

Saouji is convinced there are ways to stop this scourge. Currently, the phonelines reach the bottom of the valleys, meaning it is fairly easy for locals to stay in contact with the various trekking agencies and only have to leave their village for the duration of the job. A great example of this is Mingma Tenzi Sherpa, the new local representative of Nepalko Sathi. One of the most successful summiters in the world, Mingma Tenzi came to recognition in 2021, alongside nine other Nepalese climbers, when he became the first to summit K2 in the winter, in what was one of the greatest feats of contemporary mountaineering. His track record is impressive, having already climbed twenty-three peaks over 8,000 metres. Yet after each expedition, he returns to Gonthala, with his wife and two children, and works his land.

As an aspiring mountain guide, Tendi has been able to kill two birds with one stone. He had imagined a trekking route far from the pedestrian highways, such as the Annapurna Circuit, thus offering visitors an authentic tourist experience, right in the heart of Khembalung. At the same time, generous fundraising has allowed Nepalko Sathi to finance several projects, particularly that of offering mountain guide training to young Sherpas in the valley.

Over the years, Nepalko Sathi has managed to attach itself to a vision of long-term development in these mountain regions. For Tendi, who barely attended primary school himself in just two years, children's education is an essential part of this development. However, to do this infrastructure and trails need to be improved, especially considering most of the bridges in the area are in very poor condition. In the twenty years since Tendi, Khamsu and Saouji founded Nepalko Sathi, this forgotten valley has rediscovered a new way of living, centered on sustainable development.

It is Khamsu's dream to build several houses in Saisima to provide accommodation for nuns, visitors and for those who would agree to move back from the city to live in the country. He personally never regrets his decision to leave for Kathmandu, because it meant that his son was able go on to accomplish great things. Even so, he realizes that living conditions back in their native lands can always be improved.

CHAPTER TWENTY-EIGHT

THE TENDI SHERPA FOUNDATION

IN THE WINTER OF 2013, Jim Lang and Gordon Sutherland are in great shape. Gordon has just completed a six-week expedition in Bhutan, having explored several sectors of the Everest region beforehand. To acclimatize to the altitude, the two Scots in their fifties had both climbed Mont Blanc and Kilimanjaro, and now the friends are reflecting on another summit within their reach. Their first thought is Cho Oyu, but fear that anything over 8,000 metres is probably a bit too much for them. The next option is Mount Elbrus (5,642m), but this is dismissed because of potential political tensions with Russia and the next Olympic Games in Sochi. Instead, Aconcagua, in Argentina, seems a more natural choice, and few weeks before flying out, they complete their warm-up with three winter climbs in the Atlas Mountains.

In February, Gordon and Jim arrive in Argentina, perfectly prepared. The two men take advantage of their layover in Mendoza to stop at the best vineyards in the region and sample the famous Argentinian Malbecs. They meet Tendi for a delicious meal at the Los Penitentes Hotel, where the Scots enjoy huge mouth-watering steaks, while he tucks into a delicious vegetarian dish.

Gordon and Jim are pleased when their new guide shows a discreet yet genuine interest in their families and professional lives. He also asks them about their preparation and congratulates them after they list the mountains they have climbed during their training.

One morning, at base camp, everyone is gathered in the canteen tent when an Argentinian television crew arrives. A journalist, accompanied by a cameraman, asks to speak to Tendi, who greets the group and answers, in perfect Spanish, that he is just about to serve breakfast to his clients. The two Scots look at each other in disbelief. Outside, a TV set is hastily set up and the pair go out to watch, flabbergasted at what the journalist asks:

'Tendi Sherpa, over the years you've made it to the summit of Everest ten times. Why are you interested in climbing Aconcagua again when you've already climbed it several times before with other clients?'

Jim and Gordon cannot believe it. At no time over the past few days has Tendi told them about his previous exploits. They even feel a little ridiculous for having boasted about their own achievements. At the end of the interview, Tendi finally tells them more about himself and, good-naturedly, speaks for hours about his multiple expeditions to Everest.

The climb to Camp Canada (4,900m) progresses very smoothly. The weather is perfect; ideal for dining outside and grilling some burgers, and the two Scots even regret that a good Malbec is not on the menu. The next evening, at the upper camp of Nido de Condores, big, black clouds close in, signalling the arrival of a proper storm. The fabric of the tent threatens to tear at any moment, and the mountaineers spend a restless night with sleep seemingly impossible to find. The next morning, Tendi braves the raging elements to make sure everyone is alright, informing them in the process that some tents have been blown away and a few mountaineers have lost their lives. Consequently, with the storm forecast to continue for a few days, the decision is taken to return to base camp as quickly as possible.

As the bad weather continues, Tendi has no choice but to put an end to the whole expedition, meaning the two friends are forced to give up on their dream. They return to the UK incredibly frustrated, although the pain of missing out on the summit is lessened by the birth of a beautiful new friendship. In a nod to the story Tendi told them of his ascent up Mera Peak with his father when he was just 14 years old, the pair decide to hire him for an attempt up this 6,000-metre plus Himalayan mountain.

And so, two years later, Gordon, Jim and Tendi find themselves at the base camp of the first peak Tendi ever conquered. They arrive in a blizzard and a rescue operation is in already progress, which Tendi immediately joins and, with his great experience, takes a leadership role. Persistant bad weather forecasts push most other expeditions to give up, but Tendi encourages Gordan and Jim to be patient and, as we all know, bad weather has never made the Scottish back down. Tendi takes advantage of a thin weather window to sneak between the clouds and the ascent presents few difficulties, apart from the usual risks to be found when climbing at altitude and on glaciers. When they reach 6,470 metres, the three men are completely alone in the world. The view of the Himalayan range is breathtaking, with Everest, Lhotse, Makalu and Cho Oyu seemingly only a step away in front of them.

Until now, the two Scots had never been involved in any particular charitable cause, but having met Tendi, they soon realize that, in their own way, they have it in their power to make a difference. Since they became friends, Tendi has spoken to them at length about Nepalko Sathi, and how he still has great ambitions to develop different programmes, especially in the rural areas of his country. Together, Gordon and Jim have invaluable contacts in Scotland and England and believe they could raise funds to support Tendi's projects.

And thus the 'Tendi Sherpa Foundation' is born. Gordon and Jim are joined on the board of directors by Jeremy and Rob, two friends with extensive legal and financial skills, and the foundation is registered as a UK charity in September 2018. The first fundraising efforts are a resounding success – Tendi certainly knows how to talk to a crowd. Several expeditions are organized to help introduce the Khembalung Valley to new donors so that they can see with their own eyes what has been done with their money, as well as allowing them to see everything that still needs to be done.

The main priority is to support children in rural areas, where many still have limited access to quality education even in the twenty-first century. Too many parents prefer their children to help with household chores rather than waste time studying, which often means going to school is seen as a tedious task for many of them. So, to combat this, the four Britons manage to set up an effective scholarship system. The administrators are also fully aware of the role religion plays in Tendi's life, and the lives of everyone in his home valley. The Saisima *gompa* was partially destroyed during the earthquake that devastated Nepal in 2015, leaving large cracks in the wall. Now, the fragile structure risks being washed away by landslides during the monsoon season, and Tendi is afraid of what might happen should people continue to use it for worship. One option is to change the *gompa*'s location, which at present is far too exposed. It is the perfect opportunity to think big, with his idea being to create a community centre around the new place of prayer. More than just a temple, Tendi wants to build a centre for cultural and educational purposes, with the added possibility of teaching Sherpas and Rai children from several surrounding hamlets.

The central rooms in *gompas* are often unoccupied between ceremonies, and increased fundraising means they can finance this multifunctional centre dedicated not only to prayer, but also to school and professional education. After three years of building, the Naya Saisima centre is finally filled with flamboyant colours and positive energy, providing the opportunity for dozens of villagers to train as cooks, painters, electricians, masons and even carpenters.

Ever since the famous avalanche that hit the slopes of Everest in 2014, Tendi has strived to provide more substantial support to orphans left behind by such tragedies. Indeed, whether they are guides, summiters or simple porters, many fathers who die in the line of duty leave behind widows without any substantial income. The annuities granted by the state are derisory, meaning the courageous women often find themselves unable to offer any sort of future for their children, and sometimes cannot even manage to clothe or feed them properly. Tendi has lost many loved ones over the years; victims of avalanches, falls, altitude sickness, exhaustion, pulmonary edemas or even heart attacks, and behind each one of these is often the face of an innocent child. Most of them live in Kathmandu, which is why Tendi aims to build a school on the outskirts of the city to offer the chance for primary education. As a father himself, he knows how much his eldest daughter benefits from having good teachers.

CHAPTER TWENTY-NINE

LOOKING TO THE FUTURE

ACONCAGUA BASE CAMP OFTEN WITNESSES changes in plans, especially when the weather is bad. In 2014, Dave Schaeffer, from Colorado, is among the candidates aiming to reach the summit. Employed at a mountaineering clothing store in Denver, the company he works for knows that the best way to recommend products to their customers is to test the equipment out in the field. Arriving in Argentina alone, he has no option but to face the cold, wind, rain and snow on his own. Out of nowhere, Tendi and Dave soon start talking about how important it is to have the correct clothing, with the guide explaining the various difficulties he regularly encounters with such things.

Conditions constantly change up in the high mountains and sometimes, when the body is in motion at 7,000 metres, it can quickly become stiflingly hot in big expedition down jackets. At the same time, Tendi has often been too cold due to the strong winds that make the temperature feel much colder than it actually is. Sweating is also a danger because if the hot air is not released, the hot-cold effect is immediate. Dave takes notes, drawing diagrams, scribbling down figures and asking specific questions. The two men debate for hours. Gore-Tex, fibres, zippers, pockets and even different colours:

the topics of discussion are endless. Ever the dreamer, Tendi imagines himself running a mountaineering shop in Kathmandu between expeditions, while it turns out Dave has been thinking about becoming his own boss for some time.

The two friends weigh up their options of going into business together. Tendi would make a great model for testing out clothes in real-life conditions, but he has no money put aside to finance such a project. Instead, Dave quits his job and invests his own funds in the venture. Thanks to his great communication skills, the American approaches potential investors, who are impressed with the concept and with having Tendi as the potential 'face' of the brand. Eventually, the two friends found 'Himali', which means 'inhabitants of the Himalayan mountains' in Nepali. The letter H acts as their logo, with the graphic design forming the number fourteen (the number of peaks over 8,000 metres) as part of the letter.

As always, the early days are very complicated. You need to draw the samples, choose the materials, not to mention decide where the clothes are going to be produced. However, as budgets are limited, production is initially confined to a few T-shirts and caps. Still, less than a year after its launch, the first quilted jacket with the 'Himali' logo goes on sale on the Kickstarter website. The range naturally grows over the years and, in December 2021, before flying to Antarctica, Tendi and Dave open their first store in Boulder, Colorado, having previously only conducted sales online.

Each new season, Tendi tests out prototype outfits on top of the highest mountains in the world, noting the various corrections required as the expeditions progress. For Dave, such close collaboration is an essential part of making the business work, with one partner always needing the other to validate their decisions. Marketing-wise, Dave was absolutely right; Tendi is the perfect person to represent the brand. He regularly records videos for their website, Facebook and Instagram pages, with his face to camera routine and positive attitude triggering thousands of likes.

Whether in the United States, Argentina, Switzerland or UK, the conferences headed by Tendi are consistently full. Always honoured to be there, he throws himself into these special moments where he can share his experiences, never failing to have a blast talking about his climbs, while the long line of questions from the public can sometimes go on for hours. At the end of the meetings, people often approach him for autographs, and he is always sure to pay particular attention to each individual.

Being in the spotlight has never gone to his head. Tendi has always known how to keep his feet on the ground, which is arguably his greatest strength. As he approaches his forties, he often wonders about his future. Physically, he still feels very fit, despite some recurring tension in his neck and persistent discomfort in one knee. An osteopath he consulted in Switzerland explained that the pain was probably due to the heavy loads he carried as a teenager, when he had not quite finished growing to his full size.

Tendi knows that he is putting his body to the test, which will certainly have consequences in the future. Since the birth of Dechen, his youngest child, he has tried to limit the risks inherent in his profession. In his mind, it is clear what he needs to do; in the next ten years, he will reduce the number of climbs he undertakes before focussing on organizing and managing expeditions. He naturally wants to spend more time with his children, aware that his absences are particularly painful for

Dolma. Even though he knows his little girl is surrounded by a loving mother and grandparents, she still misses her dad very much when he goes away. Tendi would also prefer his daughters to spend less time in Kathmandu, the pollution and noise certainly not offering the best environment for them to grow and flourish.

Recently, he has spoken to Phuru of his desire to live in Saisima for a few months every year. Not immediately, of course, but when he reaches 50. On his return from a two-week stay with Saouji, in March 2022, his dream has taken on a much firmer shape. He explains to his wife that the road networks have improved considerably, with two bridges, funded by Nepalko Sathi and the Tendi Sherpa Foundation, shortening the journey considerably. Thanks to efforts to widen the routes, the paths are now passable in all seasons, including during the monsoon. On seeing the Sky Gardens, Tendi can already imagine Phuru cultivating their own vegetable patch.

His wife, a big fan of social media, will probably be able to get online in a few years' time thanks to continually improving Wi-Fi coverage in the isolated valleys. Unfortunately, for now at least, it is still the case that the village does not even have any electricity, with only a few portable solar panels providing backup energy. In almost ten years of marriage, Phuru has never been to Saisima. The opportunity has never arisen, and the girls are still too small to walk the several days required to reach the village. Consequently, she struggles to express an opinion on the subject, mainly because such a project is still only a possibility at present.

Saisima is a sacred village, which is one of the reasons why Tendi is so keen to soak in its divine ambience. His attachment to his native Khembalung is rooted in his family history, his ancestors having migrated from the Tibetan highlands to Makalu Barun National Park, in eastern Nepal, in the sixteenth century. They had fled religious tensions with the Mongols and travelled more than 2,000 kilometres to build the hamlet of Manirku, at an altitude of 2,200 metres above sea level.

In 1974, Manirku was inhabited by two Sherpa families from the Taktok tribe. Whether winter or summer, the days of these particularly pious families were spent between working in the fields and reading mantras. Khamsu, the eldest of seven children, was likewise destined to study Buddhism. One day, when visitors were rare in these isolated valleys, a monk dressed in a homespun robe appeared in the distance. The children immediately shouted, 'Look! It's Uncle Lama!'

Tendi's great-uncle, who had spent several years in a monastery, spoke to his brothers, saying 'Several days walk from here is a sacred land in the Khembalung Valley, where several Taktok already live. There's no monk there, but it's still a special place for Tibetan Buddhism. We must restore the old *gompa* and install a *lama* there.'

Turning to Tendi's grandfather, he added, 'I immediately thought of you.'

The family took an explorative journey lasting several days in the Himalayan highlands before finally reaching the last village in the valley: Saisima, an inhospitable hamlet of a few houses, established on a slope. Tendi's grandfather immediately took on the role of the new *lama*, while his great-uncle began teaching monks at the school. Later, Khamsu took over between expeditions. Today, the continuation of this deep faith is safeguarded by Nima, Tendi's younger brother, who is already on the way to becoming an important Buddhist master. Studying the sacred texts has been a priority of his since he was young. Too busy with his studies, he also missed Tendi's wedding, as well as their sister Lakpa's, not to mention the births of his nephews and nieces.

Nima is always the one missing from any family celebrations, but no one holds it against him. On the contrary, Tendi greatly admires his brother's commitment and remembers that he himself once wanted to be a priest when he was little. He knows that he is happy with his life choices. At 30 years old, whilst on the Annapurna Circuit, Nima went on a retreat lasting three years, three months, three days and three hours at a monastery in Manang. Only on one, very specific, occasion was his father able to speak to him for a few minutes, but even then it was only through a small crack. The last time Tendi saw his brother, he assured him that he could never have imagined a better life for himself. Knowing the benefits meditation can bring, Tendi often wishes he could escape from his hectic life as a guide, and although he has never been on a spiritual retreat before, he openly dreams of one day being able to do so.

Whenever Nima asks Tendi if he's happy in life, he always replies, without hesitation, 'Yes, *bhai*, little brother, very! Between my family, my spiritual journey and my profession, I'm completely and utterly happy.'

ACKNOWLEDGEMENTS

To Heather Williams, my editor, who showed unfailing enthusiasm for this project from our first contact, even though she knew little about the world of mountaineering and expeditions. She immediately understood that Tendi could be a real source of inspiration. Thank you from the bottom of my heart for placing your trust in me. I hope I have been worthy.

Thank you to Charles Hewitt of Pen & Sword Books for entrusting Heather with assessing the suitability of the project and for supporting her in her vision for its development. I could not have asked for more. Thank you to my unwavering friends PJ and Yolanda Guthrie for putting me in touch with Charles and his publishing house, which is based in your beautiful Yorkshire.

For the second time in my life, England has given me the means to achieve beautiful things: the publication of this book, of course, and earlier, when I was a young adult. In 1993 I had just missed the Swiss Matura (equivalent to the International Baccalaureate) twice. I was devastated. Desperate to become a journalist, now, in my own country, all the doors had been slammed in my face. Armed with courage, and no doubt a bit of nerve, I presented myself for an entrance exam to London South Bank University. I was successful, despite my repeated school failures and severe dyslexia, and four years later had gained my bachelor's degree in international politics and modern languages, before finally realizing the dream I had

had since I was 12: to work at RTS TV news, where I still work today. In light of this journey, I want to say a very big thank you to this United Kingdom that I love so much!

To my adored Dad, whom readers have previously discovered under the nickname of 'Saouji'. In 2016 he self-published the book *Tendi Sherpa, Higher than Everest*, but then ceded the rights to me so that I could draw inspiration from his writings in order to continue to shed light on his spiritual son, Tendi.

Tendi. Thank you for coming into my life twenty years ago and for all the wisdom you give me. I look at the world differently since I met you. You have taught me tolerance and compassion. To my delight, you are also a role model for my daughter, Romane Dali. I am forever saying to her, 'What would Uncle Tendi do if he were in your place?' I hope readers, too, will see the depth of your soul. If only the rest of humanity could be a little more like you!

Romane, my darling, I dedicate this book to you. You who were so patient during the writing of it, when I diverted time away that we could have spent together. Throughout your eleven years, you have never blamed me for anything, even when I answered, 'No, sorry darling. I have to work,' when you asked me to go skiing with you, play a game, watch a TV series, or simply go for a walk in the forest near our home.

To your father, who supported me in the writing of this book, thank you from the bottom of my heart.

Thanks to Isabelle Gonet who was, in my opinion, the most beautiful voice and the most beautiful writer at RTS. Today you are a young, active retiree who has devoted so much of your time to proofreading and correcting my manuscript. Your encouragement was invaluable and although we were not friends right away, today I count you among my most precious.

Virginie Lenk, my faithful accomplice. I hope you did not mind too much spending our weekend in Berlin correcting a manuscript that was still full of mistakes. Your strokes of the red pen have been most useful to me.

A special thank you to Maud Woiczik, a young anthropology graduate from the University of Montreal. Maud provided her knowledge and precision so that I could include the necessary details of the rites, beliefs, and the history of the Sherpas in this book. I could never have imagined this story without such scientific expertise at my side. Her help was instrumental and I wish her every success in her future anthropological work.

Peter, George and Alexander Hillary. What an honour for me to count you among my friends. I so admire the way you carry the legacy of your father and grandfather: Sir Edmund would no doubt be proud of what you are doing for the Sherpa people and the children of Nepal.

Mike Hamill. Thank you for giving me such a good picture of how Tendi does his job, and for offering him a working environment that corresponds to his ethics. You unquestionably play a key role in his life.

Nicolas Schneiter, *lama*, who helped me understand the importance of Buddha in Tendi's existence so that I now better comprehend the contribution of such a practice in his daily life. You walk the same path of awakening and radiate so much positivity. I am happy to have you both at my side.

Nicolas Bossard. Thanks to you I understood that Tendi was not quite a superhero, but a man just like any other, with all his strengths and weaknesses as well, thus making him all the more human.

Adrien Pinho. Thank you for your first external review, and for helping me return to my manuscript. You helped me put some sort of order to my chapters. In the same spirit, thank you to Sophie Cuenot for also providing an uncompromising review. Thanks to my great cycling and hiking friend, Caroline Délèze, for inviting me to look up from my computer to get some fresh air and recharge my batteries. Your many encouragements, as well as your verifications concerning the medical aspects of the book, are most welcomed.

Dave Schaeffer, Tendi's partner, who together launched the Himali range of specialist clothing. Dave was kind enough to allow us to use the cover photograph of Tendi, designed by the excellent photographer, Marshall Cody.

Thank you to all those who were kind enough to entrust me with their stories of Tendi via videoconference, telephone or email: Olya Lapina, Brian Smith, Dr Edward Dohring, Jane and Gabby Kanizay, Phuru Sherpa, Tenji Sherpa, Facundo Arana, François Mathey, Arthur Maret, Dr Alexia Willame, Keiichi Iwasaki, Jeremy Edwards, Gordon Sutherland, Rob Roger, Jim Lang, Benoît Aymon and Willie and Damian Benegas.

Finally, I offer these thanks to my family. To my adored big brother, Pierre-Armand, who dedicated hours describing the villages and pathways of the remote Nepalese valleys to me. To my big sister, Dominique, who is always full of enthusiasm when I talk to her about my projects. To Nanny and Aunt Kiki, who always take such great care of my Romane.

A very special tribute to my cousin, Estelle, who overcame a serious illness and to Uncle Pierre-Etienne, who survived this damn Covid. Through these trials you have both climbed your own Everest!

▲ ▲ ▲

For more information on the Tendi Sherpa Foundation, or to make any donations in the name of 'Higher than Everest', please visit https://www.tsfnepal.org/donations.

For more information on the Nepalkho Sathi Friends of Nepal charity, or to make any donations in the name of 'Higher than Everest', please visit https://nepalko-sathi.com/devenir-membre-2.